Inside Book Publishing
Second edition

Giles Clark

.RIFFITH COLLEGE DUBLIN
South Circular Road, Dublin 8.
Tel: 4545640. Fax: 4549265

in association with

BOOK HOUSE TRAINING CENTRE

A **BLUEPRINT** book
published by Routledge
London and New York

Journalism

First published 1988 by Blueprint
Second edition 1994
Reprinted 1995

Reprinted 1996, 1998
by Routledge
11 New Fetter Lane, London EC4P 4EE

Simultaneously published in the USA and Canada
by Routledge
29 West 35th Street, New York, NY 10001

© 1988, 1994 Giles N. Clark

Typeset in 10/12pt Palatino by
Intype, London
Printed and bound in Great Britain by
The University Press, Cambridge

British Library Cataloguing in Publication Data
A catalogue record for this book is available from the British
Library

Library of Congress Cataloging in Publication Data
A catalog record for this book is available from the Library of
Congress

ISBN 0–415–13663–6

Contents

GRIFFITH COLLEGE DUBLIN
South Circular Road, Dublin 8.
Tel: 4545640. Fax: 4549265

Preface

In the 1980s, the Society of Young Publishers (SYP) asked me to write a book for the benefit of its members, giving an overview of publishing and the careers available. My employer, The Open University, supporting the project, gave me special leave to undertake the primary research and over 150 publishing managers were interviewed.

The publishing history of this book is indicative of the dramatic and sometimes fraught changes that have since occurred in the industry. My first contract was with Allen & Unwin, a long-established, family-owned publisher of medium size and diversity most noted for its general list, including the classic works by J. R. R. Tolkien of *Lord of the Rings* and associated titles. This publisher also had a respected school textbook list, and higher education and professional titles in the earth sciences and the social sciences. By the time I had pulled together my research, Allen & Unwin had been taken over by another privately owned company and became Unwin Hyman. My first editor Adam Sisman left the restructured company (later going on to write a well received biography of A. J. P. Taylor), and my new editor cancelled my contract and paid compensation. Unwin Hyman was then bought by HarperCollins, the international book publishing imprint of Rupert Murdoch's media corporation, News International. The valuable Tolkien classics joined the ranks of other famous dead and living authors of HarperCollins, but the staff were surplus as were the more specialist titles. A few of the Unwin Hyman managers formed University College London Press and the social science titles were acquired from Harper-Collins by Routledge, the prolific and respected academic imprint of the International Thomson Organization.

I was thankfully saved from the wilderness of being unpublished by Gordon Graham, then President of The Publishers Association and Chief Executive of Butterworths (legal and technical publishers) who introduced me to Dag Smith of the Book House Training Centre who contacted Blueprint Publishing – a new small publisher spearheaded and owned by Charlotte Berrill who successfully focused on books on publishing and printing. My work was adapted to the brief they drew up. The first edition of *Inside Book Publishing* (1988) was energetically published and sold by Blueprint.

Blueprint Publishing was later acquired by Chapman & Hall, the scientific and professional book imprint of Thomson. In 1993, Vivien James (the publisher in charge of Blueprint) asked me for a thoroughly revised second edition, which duly appeared in the autumn of 1994. During the summer of 1995, International Thomson conducted a re-organization which included combining the business and management lists of Routledge and Chapman & Hall into a new company, the International Thomson Business Press, and the transference of Blueprint to the media studies list of Routledge under the editorship of Rebecca Barden. By the autumn of 1995 the first printing of the second edition of *Inside Book Publishing* had fortuitously sold out, enabling the reprint to appear under the Routledge banner.

Thus since conception, my work has passed through four changes of outright publishing ownership and five imprints and editors over a decade. This story is not unique in publishing today.

My special thanks are therefore due on the first edition to all my friends in the SYP, to The Open University, Gordon Graham, Dag Smith and Charlotte Berrill; and on the second edition to Vivien James, to Liz Farrant for compiling the Appendix on publishing courses, to Iain Brown for 'Further Reading' and particularly to Audrey N. Clark for reading the manuscript and indexing. Furthermore I am indebted to the many dozens of people who have helped me with *Inside Book Publishing* over the years.

About the author

Giles Clark, with a family background in publishing, works at The Open University, Milton Keynes, where he is Deputy Managing Editor in the Book Trade Department, Publishing Services. He organizes co-publication arrangements between the University and a wide range of publishers from small to large, across most academic disciplines. The partnerships forged with commercial publishers extend the University's readership internationally, reduce its costs and give it entrepreneurial income. He also develops the University's best-selling own-published titles. In a private capacity, he facilitates the publishing of books of local interest to serve the community. Over the past 15 years he has made an extensive study of all aspects of commercial publishing at home and abroad.

Introduction

The aims of this book are twofold: first to give a broad overview of the activities of book publishers – to many, including authors, wrapped in myth and mystery; second to help those seeking their first job in the industry or wanting to enhance their career prospects. It should be stressed that the subject-matter relates to a highly competitive business concerned with developing and marketing books, and information, for profit, and this includes the university presses operating along similar lines. Commercial publishing is not a slow-paced genteel hobby to nurture literature or poetry without reference to the market, or a continuance of academic study, or a vehicle to express and propagate one's own particular views. Risk-taking is inherent in the business: while prepared for failures, a publisher, as an eternal optimist with a short memory, forever searches for and expects success – sure in the belief that future rewards will more than exceed past losses.

Publishing involves working with (but not universally for) congenial people and provides opportunity for individuality, creativity, and considerable responsibility for the young. The work-force is fluid, there are many possibilities for changing jobs early on, scope to go freelance, and for some high-fliers, the building of empires. Even quite junior jobs call for the management of people, products and money. Such skills combined with ideas, effective communication and organization are marketable.

Starting salaries are low, staff work hard and long hours, formal career structures are opaque, senior salaries are usually modest, and there is little job security in some firms. Yet there is intense competition to secure even the most junior jobs, and many people are hooked for much of their working life. The appeal and fulfilment lie in serving people's entertainment, educational and informational needs, and sometimes in influencing the future course of events, in discovering and moulding new writing talent, in creating new markets. Publishers are continually dealing with many new products, each of which presents its own challenge in the way it can be produced and marketed for a particular audience. All jobs include routine and boring work. It is the infinite variety that fascinates. Each book presents its own problems to be solved. And success depends on personal contacts with authors, illustrators, printers, customers and colleagues.

'To publish' is commonly defined as 'to make public'. Here we are concerned predominantly with the work of commercial book publishing as distinct from that of newspaper and magazine publishing.

The book is an enduring medium through which ideas and knowledge are communicated, and a society's culture portrayed; and as such it is a prime resource for the student, the general reader and the media. The diversity of books and publishers is vitally important to a democracy.

The book scores over other communications media by its length, permanence, portability, robustness, re-readability, accessibility, overall general convenience, physical attractiveness, status in society and relative cheapness. It has no need for a power source, an after-sales service or maintenance and, unlike electronic media, it transcends ever-changing and dating technologies. Book publishing, as a long-established industry, has a worldwide distribution system through which its output can be traded profitably on a continuing and largely regulated and controlled basis; but while book publishers have to compete vigorously against other forms of entertainment, other learning processes and information sources, they are in a strong position to take advantage of emerging electronic media markets.

Book publication attracts an enormous number of diverse authors who want to communicate their ideas, thereby gaining recognition. Book publishing serves the million-copy fiction writer and the most specialist author with under one thousand sales: books can be published profitably for tiny markets which though limited in scale are limitless in number.

Elements underpinning UK book publishing are copyright protection; a plethora of talented living (and dead) authors; the freedom to publish; the English language, fortunately shared by much of the world; and a multiplicity of varied micro-markets, as opposed to a few mass markets, that arise and change rapidly and give opportunities for a wide range of publishers.

Publishers are not mere 'middlemen' interjecting themselves between authors and readers. They commission authors (often before manuscripts are written), confer authority and add value to authors' works, finance the multiplication of copies, and promote and sell the works wherever possible. The publisher, aiming to make a profit for the owners/shareholders and to carry on publishing:

- researches in the markets in which it specializes and builds contacts;
- seeks authors (sometimes in competition with other publishers) and is sought by them;
- matches marketable ideas to saleable authors;
- assesses the quality of the author's work (sometimes externally refered), costs of production and sales prospects;
- decides whether to risk its investment funds in particular authors/projects to appear under its imprint;
- edits and designs books to meet author/market needs;
- specifies, buys and oversees the work of print suppliers (in the UK or abroad) which manufacture the books;
- builds a worldwide sales network;
- promotes and publicizes the books to their intended users, the media, and to the intermediaries (the retailers, wholesalers, and overseas firms) through which the books are mainly sold;
- sells the books face-to-face to the intermediaries;
- holds bulk stocks of titles to satisfy demand;
- fulfils orders, distributes the books and collects the money, paying royalties to authors on sales made.

Additional income benefiting publisher and author may be made from various rights sales which enable other firms at home and abroad to exploit the author's work in different ways, media and languages.

Although the specialist staff of large publishers carry out all the above activities, some work (such as the detailed editing of books) is often contracted out to freelance workers or possibly to other firms. Smaller publishers may not have the resources to employ their own sales representatives or to distribute the books themselves so they may use larger publishers, or specialist firms. Apart from the decision to publish a book and raising the finance, all the other work could conceivably be carried out, under the publisher's direction, by freelances or separate firms. But there are potential drawbacks: the publisher may have less control over the way the books are produced, lose the marketing emphasis projected by its own employees committed solely to its books, and contribute to profit margins of sub-contractors.

Publishers, of course, come in all shapes and sizes; but in order to give a comprehensive review this book concentrates on commercial publishing in medium and large firms with their specialist departments. Such firms account for most of the industry's sales. Small publishers are generally started up by people with particular expertise: the information contained here, covering the way in which larger firms with more resources tackle other areas, could be invaluable to them.

The industry was traditionally broadly based with many medium-sized firms, but by the mid-1980s and after a spate of mergers and acquisitions, ownership became far more concentrated. A handful of very large international publishing groups now control over half the home market, and the breadth of choice for both authors and employees is narrowing.

Chapter 1 'Book publishers: from family houses to international media corporations', traces significant changes in the structure of publishing businesses and the market to the present day. The chapter looks forward to the emerging electronic media markets that may open new opportunities for book and learned journal publishers.

Negative impacts of the take-overs of smaller publishers include the cancellation of authors' contracts, staff redundancies and in some cases the virtual demise of once respected imprints. On the other hand, some bought firms survive relatively intact, are rejuvenated, and take full advantage of corporate funds, management expertise, lower print production costs and greater worldwide marketing muscle provided by the larger enterprise. Some authors, too, benefit from increased sales and higher royalties on sales made by the constituent firms of an international group.

A sign of a vigorous industry is the frequent start-up of new firms – compared with many industries publishing needs only a little equipment (e.g. a personal computer) and a relatively small amount of investment capital. Some new firms arise from management buy-outs of lists or imprints surplus to a large firm; or are created afresh from their former employees. No professional qualifications are needed to be a publisher – entry is unrestricted.

While the trend is towards larger publishers, there will always be room for numerous innovative, imaginative and entrepreneurial small publishers which, with lower overheads, can move faster and more sharply than some large ones that are overburdened with bureaucracy and unresponsive to innovation and to fast changing markets. Small publishers tend to be more specific in the books they publish, and with less resources and small margin of error, must work hard at choosing and marketing their titles carefully, and at developing authors and backlist books. They can offer a more personal service to authors, who may receive scant attention from larger publishers.

All publishers give most attention to their most important new books, especially in respect of marketing and sales effort. An author, or book, ranked lowly on a large publisher's list may be given greater prominence on a smaller publisher's. Small publishers may, however, ultimately lose their successful authors to larger publishers.

Publishing is intimately interwoven with society, touches on every aspect of knowledge, often reaches a worldwide market and produces books for tiny tots to high-powered lawyers. But publishers specialize in marketing certain kinds of books, the main sectors of which are described in Chapter 2.

Fundamentally book publishing rests on copyright and the creativity of authors. Chapter 3 'From author contract to market outlet', opens with a review of the importance of copyright and gives an example of the contractual relationship between author and publisher. Most publishers do not sell their books directly to readers. Publishers' main customers are the booksellers and others in the supply chain. The ever-widening sales channels making books available to the public in the UK are summarized.

Whatever the size, a publisher's underlying strength lies in the quality of its staff: a group of individuals who, ideally, share similar aims and values and are committed to the core business of publishing and selling books and information, who establish a stable of authors and go from strength to strength over the years. Publishing is a complex interplay of the creative and economic.

The publication of a book is a complex activity demanding at every stage ideas, flexibility and great attention to detail, and the close liaison of many specialist staff from editorial through to sales and distribution. Chapter 4 'The process and the people', outlines the principal tasks performed, generally concurrently, by staff in various departments. The main skills ideally needed to perform the tasks are listed, but it would be a rare person indeed who was strong in all.

Chapter 5 concentrates on the central financial aspects of publishing a book, which in itself is a new and different business venture, and Chapter 6 offers career advice.

Such a broad survey necessarily excludes much detail but it should give you insight of what is to many an exciting and satisfying way of life.

SALIENT FEATURES OF BOOK PUBLISHING

By commercial standards, book publishing as a whole is a small but profitable and influential industry which turns over more than £2.2 billion and is thought to employ around 14 000–20 000 people. Detailed statistics on employment structure or salaries are not available, though it is estimated that full-time job losses at the peak of the recession in the early 1990s were around 10% of the work force. However, there were very few outright company failures. Publishing companies can usually generate high turnover with relatively small numbers of full-time employees. Whitaker lists 2500 'most active' publishers but this includes many small publishers and those for which publishing is a sideline.

Compared with other industries book publishing is unparalleled in the number of new products launched each year. In 1993, 62 102 new books were published in the UK, up from 45 652 in 1987, 37 382 in 1980, and 27 247 in 1975. In 1988 the number of titles in print was 444 000; by 1993 it had reached 600 000. It is predicted, on current growth patterns, that by the year 2000 annual new title output will surpass 100 000. It should be noted that these statistics include books originated in the USA but published in the UK, especially in the academic and professional fields, and those produced by thousands of small publishers or 'non-profit publishers'. However, in 1993, for example, Whitaker Bibliographic Services recorded a further 20 922 'new editions' and they include many books re-issued in paperback or merely repackaged by commercial houses. Generally speaking the number of copies sold has not grown apace. Print quantities per title have declined, and the expected effective sales life of titles has shortened, often to under a year.

Critics of book publishers perennially complain about publishers' 'over-production' of new books; that so many new books, they argue, do not allow sufficient advertising or bookshop display of each one; that by publishing fewer books, better books (even though such a term could be subjectively defined) would result. But would, for example, a fiction publisher qualitatively improve the work of current great writers by publishing fewer new writers, or would it by publishing fewer third-rate writers cause more of them to turn into second-raters, and second-raters into first-raters? Would the curtailment of academic publishing aid poetry publishing? A publisher could ask each editor to cut the number of new books signed up with a view to sharpening the editors' judgement of quality or somehow to reducing their fallibility. If that were possible a publisher could increase its sales and reputation by critically reducing the size of its list every year. Some publishers (particularly during recessions) cut their lists and may claim that they increase sales, while others continue to expand title output and may claim that they are increasing their market share. Authors want to be published. Publishers constantly try to find new ones, and meet the ever growing diverse leisure and professional interests of readers; and there is fierce competition between publishers in every field. New title output and reader choice increases.

For company size, each publisher annually launches a large number of untried and untested products. Few new books could support the cost of retaining a market-research company to pretest the market; thus their publishing is a high-risk decision. Books like any commodity need a clear perception of the product and buyer and vigorous marketing to bring them together, but the marketing techniques deployed by other consumer goods industries are not wholly appropriate. Books are not a basic life necessity; the reader usually buys a single copy, only once, not repeatedly; company brand name identification, with some exceptions, is of little consequence to the reader (but can be important to booksellers); and readers are confronted by a multiplicity of choices to satisfy their interests. Books are borrowed free from libraries and from other sources (about 33% of the population are active library users and perhaps an additional 25% are occasional users). Library users are good book buyers. It usually takes a long time to produce a book from manuscript to bound copy – about 4–12 months (or more) – and to allow adequate time for worldwide promotion and sales. Most of a publisher's cash is tied up in stock. The turnover of a publisher's complete stock of all books commonly takes more than a year. Typically 20% of the titles account for 80% of the revenue but the uncertainties of estimating demand make the success of such books initially difficult to determine. Publishers service an enormous number of small orders, often of low value, but totalling considerable sums.

The publishers that prosper in good times and bad are those which have developed and maintained a core group of long life titles delivering handsome margins, which are not too overdependent on such past successes and which focus on producing high quality books which are good of their kind. Provided a project has a genuine reason for being, reflects quality in its conception, content and production, and is made available at the right time and price to a well-targeted market it will sell, sometimes prodigiously. Many of the most interesting and successful books are those that are exceptional, not a slavish imitation of other books or even a product of market research.

Much of UK publishing depends for its survival on exporting. Around 30% of UK publishers' sales are exports and additionally publishers receive royalties from editions licensed abroad. (Exports are nearly double imports.) The major markets are the countries of mainland Europe (36%), North America (18%) and Australasia (10%). From the mid-1980s to the early 1990s, sales to mainland Europe grew and supplanted North America as the main export destination, and sales to Australasia declined. East Asian and Asia/Pacific rim countries are growing in importance.

UK industry exports approach those of the much larger US industry. Both countries dominate English language exports, but face increasing competition from German, Dutch, and indigenous Asian publishers, some of which publish in English. Third World piracy is a considerable threat and is the enemy of UK publishers, legitimate indigenous publishers and authors alike. The growth of the bulk photocopying industry, especially in the Middle East and the Far East, hinders exports. The British Council is the major government agency promoting books, journals, electronic publications and authors abroad.

Cost breakdown

An author may say to a publisher's editor: 'I'm writing the book, yet you're paying me a royalty of only 10% of the published price on copies sold ... What's happening to the remaining 90%?'. At first sight it seems grossly unfair especially when some authors may receive royalties as low as 2–3% on certain sales and take hundreds, if not thousands of hours, to write their books. Apart from the few, very successful authors, authors' earnings are rather meagre – many, probably the majority, receive less than £5000 per book, sometimes far less. If authors were paid even a reasonable hourly rate, most books would be so expensive that no copies would be sold. Instead, their earnings, like those of publishers, are derived from sales made.

The process that makes books available relies on the interaction of a wide range of companies all employing staff and trying to make a profit. A large slice of a book's published price is taken by the retailers, the publisher's main customers. To facilitate sales, they receive discounts off the book's published price (generally in the range from 20 to 55%, depending on the type of book and importance of customer). Publishers pay printers and paper suppliers for the costs of manufacturing the books (roughly 12–20% of the published price). The publisher pays royalties to authors, fees to illustrators etc., and from the remainder tries to cover its own staff and operating costs. The publisher alone takes the risk that the book may be a financial failure, as indeed many are.

Book publishers: from family houses to international media corporations

Book publishing was traditionally broadly based with many medium-sized firms employing around 50 or so staff and issuing, say, several hundred titles per year, usually in hardback. The publishers were owned privately, usually by family members who held majority share stakes. They concentrated on fiction and non-fiction (termed 'general' or 'trade' or, more recently, 'consumer books') though they also developed educational (i.e. school textbook) and academic lists, subservient to the general side.

Throughout the 1960s and 1970s (other than in the recession of the early to mid-1970s), much of the publishers' fast growing prosperity was based on readers' affluence and increasing public expenditure. The consumer book publishers of hardback adult and children's books were underpinned by generous government funding of libraries, as were the rapidly expanding educational publishers, and the academic publishers responding to heady growth in higher education. Expansion in science, technology and medicine (STM), and ample funding of university libraries stimulated the publishing of high-priced academic monographs and of immensely profitable learned journals, produced especially by the STM book publishers. During this period many of the main educational, academic and STM publishers moved out of London to cheaper offices in the New Town ring in order to house their burgeoning staff numbers.

While the first overseas subsidiaries had been opened in the late nineteenth and early twentieth centuries in Australia and Canada, in the 1960s the educational and academic houses opened subsidiaries in the newly formed African Commonwealth countries and exported massive quantities of UK-based textbooks. The Commonwealth countries' educational systems were based on UK curricula or examinations, and many professors were UK-educated.

The British publishers enjoyed their traditional export markets: the USA, Commonwealth and northern Europe. The giant American publishers with their much larger home market gave little emphasis to exports, the major exception being the college textbook publishers (especially in STM). These opened subsidiaries in the UK after the Second World War and came subsequently to dominate the English language major 'first-year' textbook adoption markets worldwide, Commonwealth countries included.

Mass-market paperback publishing grew substantially and was carried out by separate firms which in the main acquired reprint paperback rights from the famous general firms that originated titles in hardback. Literary agents who increasingly began to represent the interests of fiction and non-fiction authors, were resented by some traditional publishers who saw them as unwarranted intruders into the publisher/author relationship. New publishers arose producing in large quantities highly-illustrated non-fiction books in full colour at low and affordable prices – these books were variously described by traditionalists as 'down-market' or as 'non-books'. The publication of *The Reader's Digest Great World Atlas* (1961) with its opening of double-page spreads displaying superb full-colour graphics, with extended captions not unlike magazines, and the *Treasures of Tutankh-amun* (tied-in to the British Museum exhibition) (1972) were inspirational to some embryonic book packagers. The packagers went on to produce highly illustrated full-colour information books which they pre-sold to publishers around the world to market and distribute under the publishers' imprints. In the late 1970s, the highly illustrated publishers broke colour books into the supermarkets by producing 'own brand' books for them at very low prices.

By the end of the 1970s the era of the 'gentleman' publisher was fast disappearing. (The phrase 'gentleman' has been used historically to describe grand publishers of literary fiction or belles lettres, or derided as gentlemen who ran their companies by the seat of their pants, who adopted a paternalist management style, or who according to some literary agents exhibited very ungentlemanly behaviour indeed in their contractual arrangements with authors.) Some of the foremost publishers who had personally built great publishing companies had reached the end of their careers. Some of their descendants, given senior management positions, were either incompetent or quite ill-prepared for the changes to come.

The stable and expansionary publishing world of the 1960s and 1970s was rudely shattered by the recession of 1980 which forced publishers to cut their lists and overheads (e.g. by making redundant the older staff and the weaker staff sucked in during the fast growth era). From then on progressive cuts in public expenditure throughout the English-speaking world would be the order of the day. Reductions in public expenditure adversely affected the publishing and availability of some kinds of books, such as hardback fiction written by new and minor authors destined for public libraries, certain categories of children's books supported by public and school libraries, high-priced academic monographs for university libraries, and school textbooks produced for underfunded UK state schools. A further factor of the 1980s and early 1990s was high book-price inflation and the appreciation of sterling against the currencies of countries to which UK publishers traditionally exported. This led to a relative and slow decline in export sales and aided competition from the US publishers. For instance, American general books, particularly mass-market paperbacks and college textbooks, were more competitively priced in mainland Europe and Australia. Both US and UK textbook publishers' export sales suffered from the near collapse of Third World economies, especially the African.

The 1980s was the period of mergers and acquisitions which restructured the publishing industry. A handful of large international publishing groups eventually came to control over half the home market: long established medium-sized firms were to become a rarity. The deregulation of the financial markets led to increased availability of long- and short-term equity and debt financing allowing large publishers or their parents to take over medium-sized publishers, and small publishers to expand or start-up. Book publishing was attractive to investors who could see that the industry had consistently, that is until 1987, returned pre-tax profits and return on capital above the average level of all industries.

At an earlier time some industrial conglomerates had begun to buy up and amass publishing companies of different types (e.g. general hardback and mass-market paperback, educational, academic and STM) though they tended to keep such companies as separate, sometimes prestigious entities rather than parts of an overall corporate industrial logic. Unlike today, book publishing had traditionally been linked to printing. Some book publishers either owned printers or were owned by printers. The idea that general book publishing was part of the larger media leisure industry evolved slowly. Early examples included the acquisition of general publishers by magazine publishers and by independent television companies which wanted to control television tie-in books (the BBC usually licensed its best-selling television series tie-ins to publishers).

CONSUMER BOOK PUBLISHING

The 1980s restructuring of UK book publishing affected all types of publishing but its effects were most dramatic in consumer book publishing, the fault lines having appeared in the 1970s. As mentioned above, the ownership and character of consumer book publishing (both adult and children's) was traditionally divided between many hardback publishers and separate mass-market paperback houses. (The so-called mass-market in publishing terms ranges from the big authors who sell in mass-market paperback hundreds of thousands of copies down to minimum print runs of 25 000 copies in the 1970s, subsequently reduced to nearly half that number in the 1990s.)

The underlying publishing strategy was (and still is) to first publish and establish a book in hardback at a high price and subsequently to re-issue it, a year later or less, in a paperback format at a lower price in greater numbers to a wider audience. Hardback fiction and non-fiction lists were, and to some extent still are, published in half-yearly seasons (the spring/summer, and autumn/winter) headed by major 'lead titles' and sold to booksellers, to libraries (mainly via library suppliers) and sometimes to book clubs. Whereas the mass-market paperbacks are fast-moving, small 'A format' or 'pocket' or 'rack-sized' books published in monthly batches, each month headed by lead fiction and non-fiction titles, with various category titles forming the remainder. Such paperbacks are usually straight reductions of original hardback sizes (i.e. pages of the hardback edition are photographically reduced down to the size of the paperback edition), are printed overall in much larger quantities on cheap paper, reach a wider retail market beyond bookshops and are sold in a way more akin to that of magazines.

The respective character of hardback and paperback publishers was very different. The hardback general publishers inhabited their fine but slowly decaying Georgian houses in Bloomsbury, around Bedford Square, and in other high-class central London locations. The palatial former reception rooms, with Adam marble fireplaces and hung with chandeliers, were impressive settings for the managing director or the editorial director. The editors were very much in control. The production staff who hired the printers to produce the books, and the marketing and sales staff, were crammed in the former secondary bedrooms and servants' quarters, the basement and the attics. The mass-market paperback reprinters occupied concrete office blocks in cheaper London locations. Theirs was a sales-driven operation.

The hardback publishers played their traditional role of nurturing new writing talent and working closely with authors on manuscripts. Their backlists were complete with great and loyal authors, and some enduring money-spinning books. Their formidable reputation ensured that their new books were reviewed (literary review editors ignored paperbacks), that the public librarians would automatically order sufficient quantities, and that the compliant independent booksellers would display and stock their titles. The advent of book clubs supplied another outlet. The booksellers complained that the book clubs by offering new hardbacks at considerable discounts by mail-order were undermining their business. The publishers were pleasantly surprised by the paradoxical increased sales through bookshops stemming from a book club's large-scale consumer advertising campaigns. However, by the early to mid-1980s, hardback publishers found themselves making hardly any profit from selling copies themselves. They derived their profit and laid off risks by making rights and co-edition sales to others: to the paperback publishers, to book clubs, to US publishers and foreign language publishers etc. While the hardback publishers employed highly talented editors, some of whom had immense egos and a passion for books, they included editors who favoured pet projects and authors who produced books which few wanted to buy.

The false dichotomy between hardback and paperback publishing could not survive. The book market was rapidly changing, readers' expectations were altering, competition between publishers to secure best-selling authors was intensifying and literary agents were far more adept in extracting from publishers maximum advance payments against future royalties for their authors' works.

The hardback publishers were used to acquiring the exclusive right to publish an author's work for the full term of copyright in hardback and paperback, even though they had no mass-market paperback publishing capability, and similarly to acquiring US rights which they in turn licensed to US publishers. The hardback publisher would then sub-license the UK paperback publisher, for a fixed period (say eight years), the right to publish the paperback on which it would pay the hardback publisher a royalty of say 7.5% on published price, rising to 10% or more after specified large quantities had been sold. The hardback publisher would share the royalties received with the author (e.g. 50/50, 30/70 respectively). The paperback publisher would want to acquire its main titles two years ahead of paperback publication. The originating publisher would secure at that time a large advance payment from the paperback publisher, similarly shared with the author.

Paperback publishers facing escalating reprint advances increased their output of original titles, sometimes licensing rights to hardback publishers. In that some authors derived most of their income from paperback sales (and sometimes US sales), it was prudent for agents to cut out the hardback publisher's royalty share from such sales. Agents, for example, might license the book directly to an independent hardback publisher, to a separate paperback publisher, and to a US publisher, thereby obtaining advances from each party and full royalty rates for their authors (less the agent's commission). The general publishers which came to own both hardback and paperback firms (termed vertically integrated) paid authors full royalty rates on each edition and were therefore better positioned to capture the leading authors. Paperback and hardback publishers without a hardback or paperback arm were increasingly desperate – sometimes they entered into alliances in order to bid for the big books jointly.

Another strand leading to the amalgamation of consumer book publishing, again reaching back to the late 1970s, was the weakening polarization between the traditional formats. The mass-market paperbackers, with increasing competition between themselves, as well as higher title output, recorded lower unit sales per title. Paperback prices rose and the ownership of paperback houses became more concentrated. Furthermore readers' expectations created a new market for certain books and authors to be published in 'quality' or 'trade paperback' or 'B format' books printed in larger size to higher standards, and published in quantities lower overall than the 'A format' but at higher prices, mainly for the bookshop. Such books could be reprints from hardbacks, reissues or originals. Both mass-market paperback and hardback houses started up trade paperback literary imprints (publishing titles in monthly batches or less regularly) and some hardback houses ventured into the 'A format' field as well, usually with near fatal consequences. Over time, the use of the trade paperback to publish original fiction (including new writers) and non-fiction has grown apace.

By the end of the 1980s and early 1990s, most of the formerly independent hardback houses were part of the major publishing corporations. Each had the capability of publishing in all formats, mass-market paperback, trade paperback and hardback. Their imprints were gathered together in modern London offices usually under one roof. The new owners combed through the old reprint paperback contracts entered into by their hardback publishers with the paperback publishers and noted the titles which had, from other take-overs, fallen into the hands of rival paperback imprints and the termination dates of such licences. In due course they would claw-back the paperback rights to those books for their own paperback imprints much to the consternation of the bereft paperback reprinters, and some authors and agents.

The main financial assets of a publishing company (other than buildings etc.) are its intellectual property rights (IPR). These are enshrined in the contracts it holds with suppliers (i.e. contracts negotiated directly with authors or via their agents; book packagers, US publishers and foreign languages publishers) and with companies to which it has sold rights, such as to book clubs, US publishers and foreign language publishers, newspaper, magazine, film and television companies etc. The pressure to control rights internationally prompted US general publishers to acquire UK imprints, and vice-versa, and both UK and US publishers were attractive to expansionist mainland European publishers.

The hardback general book publishers had taken years to develop, held valuable IPR, had an increasing rarity value and at the peak of the merger boom commanded high prices.

As for the staff of the taken-over general publishers, the outlook for many was rather bleak. Other than the staff made immediately redundant, those who were transferred entered the world of corporate publishing. The editors, especially, who had been brought up in the culture of smaller companies who had enjoyed considerable autonomy in their publishing decisions over the kinds of books they wanted to publish and their work with authors, carried with them a set of values quite often at odds with their new employers who emphasized sales and profit motives and sometimes clean and tidy desks clear of manuscripts and books, a world apart from their former houses. Some editors blamed the accountants for preventing them from doing the books they wanted to publish. It was not the accountants *per se*; the publishing socio-economic culture had changed. Editorial status was no longer conferred by access to the cellar of fine wines, but by the size of their work stations. The nature of consumer book publishing had changed from being 'product-led' to being 'market-driven'. Furthermore, some publishers have the ability of leading the market by introducing new authors, publishing books in different formats, and marketing and selling them in different ways. Editorial individuality and innovation are still present in the large corporations.

Although consumer book publishing appears to be dominated by the existing majors, there are quite large publishers, for example in the highly illustrated information book field, medium-sized independents, fast-growing new entrants, and many dozens of smaller specialist publishers producing adult or children's books. Furthermore, book packagers constantly arise, pre-selling adult and children's books to publishers. The smaller publishers and book packagers cannot compete against the large corporations in terms of advances paid to agented, established authors. Thus, for example, they concentrate on bringing forward new writers, or those overlooked who may not have agents, or they build a stable of authors who will work for one-off fees instead of royalties – common in the highly illustrated book fields.

While general or 'consumer book' publishing was being restructured, the increased availability of finance in the 1980s also aided the transformation and concentration of UK bookselling. Traditionally, UK bookselling had been characterized by the existence of the major chain (which had its roots in station bookstalls and high-street stationery outlets), smaller independently owned chains and a great number of independent and small bookshops. The expansion of the major chain and the arrival of new chains established large well-stocked bookshops throughout the country. The enhanced professionalism in bookselling spread to the existing larger independents which had to compete. The small independents lost market share. The new chains aggressively expanded, opening new large shops in good, off-prime site locations but also argued with publishers that they needed higher discounts (i.e. the bookseller's percentage margin between the retail price of a book and the price bought from the publisher) and longer credit periods (i.e. the time to settle invoices) to operate. The consumer book publishers benefited from the new well-stocked and attractive bookshops displaying their books, but they gave them better discounts and credit. The power relationship between publishers and booksellers, for so long weighted in the publisher's favour, began to tip towards the major retailers, as is common in most consumer goods industries.

Another factor impinging on consumer book publishers' margins, pushing up the average discount on sales made to UK customers, was the rise of the trade wholesalers supplying the declining and fragmented independent bookshop sector. From the early 1980s to 1990s, a proportion of a publisher's sales passing through such wholesalers grew from say 10% to 20% at the expense of direct supply to bookshops. While the new and growing bookselling chains argued for discounts from the publishers of above 40% off the published price, the small independents were stuck with the traditional discounts of 33–35%. The trade book wholesalers argued they needed at least a 15% margin between the price they bought the books from the publisher and the price they sold them to an independent, thus they pressed for a 50% discount or more from the publisher.

Prior to the recession of the early 1990s, the major publishers (who started calling themselves players, invariably big players), locked themselves into a battle of paying rocketing levels of advances for lead titles in order to maintain or increase their market share of the limited number of such titles available. By the time those books were published, the consumer book market was declining. The return of unsold books from booksellers, a long-time feature of consumer book publishing (especially of paperbacks), surpassed more than 25% of the publishers' sales as booksellers destocked hardbacks and paperbacks. On some lead titles, the actual sales fell far short of the expected number on which the author's advance against royalties had been calculated – the advance was thus unearned. A publisher which may have budgeted an author's royalty rate of between 15–20% of the publisher's revenue, may have paid an advance which equated to an effective royalty rate of 30% of sales, or more in disastrous cases. The level of authors' advances and booksellers' extended credit would have to be brought under control. The consumer book publishers emerged from the recession leaner and fitter – three hour publishing lunches had been curtailed – but with low levels of profitability. However, by 1993 UK sales in real terms were beginning to pick up.

Children's publishing

By the late 1970s the outlook for some publishers of children's books, especially those producing quality hardbacks, appeared grim. Many bookshops other than the major multi-product/ stationery chain were hardly enthusiastic buyers, public and school libraries (traditional major markets) were cutting back, and the birth rate was forecast to fall. In that the vitality of children's publishing creates the book buyers of the future, there were serious worries about the end of book reading, foreshadowing the end of publishing itself. Between 1981 and 1990 the population of five- to fourteen-year-olds did indeed fall by 13% but the inventiveness of authors and illustrators, of the existing publishers (other than those which closed or sold off their imprints), of new publishers and book packagers transformed children's publishing during the 1980s into arguably the most dynamic sector of the industry. Retail sales per child rose by nearly three-times, and the number of new books and new editions (including reprints and re-issues in paperback) increased from 3009 to 5879. The sales of children's book publishers from 1985 to 1990 rose in real terms by 26% while their adult general book publishing counterparts managed only 7%.

The publishers found new ways of reaching the home market via supermarkets (from the mid-1980s selling them books appearing under the supermarket's own brand label), toyshops and direct selling distributors/book clubs etc. They sold international co-editions to US and European publishing partners, enabling picture books and highly-illustrated non-fiction or information books to be published at low and affordable prices worldwide. Paperback sales grew enormously and in volume terms came to dominate the market. Teenage fiction lists were established.

The recession of the early 1990s saw a reversal in sales of around 13% yet the publishers continued to increase their title output. Nevertheless, predicted rises in the birth rate may favour renewed home market expansion, supermarkets are taking titles on a non-exclusive basis (rather than just under their own exclusive brand label), the changes in the school market offer further prospects for the children's publishers to gain leisure and classroom sales, and there might be additional sales channels to be explored at home and overseas.

NON-CONSUMER BOOK PUBLISHING

The main publishing groups encompass the educational, academic, STM (scientific, technical and medical), learned journal and professional book publishing companies, and the two major university presses are very active in these fields. In that the main publishing sectors vary in profitability at different times, management try to spread their portfolios of companies in the UK and abroad. Some private-sector publishing groups are more weighted towards the consumer market while others are weighted in the more specialized areas. The latter, especially publishers producing high-level books and associated information and reference products for professionals (e.g. in STM, business and law), are highly profitable and strongly cash generative.

Educational publishing

During the 1980s, school pupil rolls declined, and the number of significant educational publishers decreased from around 30 to 15. Sales volumes fell from 1986 to 1990 reflecting in part the gross underfunding of UK state schools, the poverty of some Commonwealth countries and the more nationalist approaches abroad to curricula diminishing export sales. By the early 1990s, the top three publishers commanded 50% of sales to schools, the top seven over 75%. The remaining publishers concentrated in specialist areas or subjects.

The home market used to be characterized by little central government intervention and a variety of examination boards setting curricula. A diversity of books and ancillary materials were published by a variety of publishers. The books were purchased through local authorities and supplied to schools via specialist suppliers, local authority purchasing organizations and bookshops. However, the effects of the 1988 Education Reform Act were profound. The new National Curriculum was far more prescriptive and defined. At first, the publishers tried to salvage their old backlist textbooks (from which they earned most of their profits) as best they could. Nevertheless many of their products were obsolete. The race was on to produce new materials, especially schemes or programmes of study in core subjects, quickly and at great cost. Speed and quality were of the essence as each school had to be locked into the publisher's programme ideally for say three to five years. Slow publishers risked being knocked out, as indeed some were.

The government responded to the campaign mounted especially by the Educational Publishers Council, for increased school funding but only in the short-term; the sales in the early 1990s rebounded to their 1986 levels as did the publishers' profitability. Moreover, the local management of schools gave schools cheque books enabling them to order books themselves; and schools turned out to be faster payers than local authorities. Many in the former supply chain thought that publishers' distribution systems could never cope with supplying books directly to so many schools. They were wrong. Direct supply by publishers grew fast from 15% to over 45%. While publishers gave schools, if necessary, initial incentive discounts in order to secure their programmes, subsequent orders were supplied at full price or at low discounts. The publishers thus maintained their former discount levels and the direct supply route provided valuable marketing information to help fend off competitors.

The publishing of English Language Teaching (ELT) course books and other materials engages large investments and a worldwide marketing strength. By the early 1990s this expansionary and important export-orientated field was concentrated among five major publishers, including the two main university presses. The surviving publishers recognized early on that ELT

publishing was a distinct field needing its own publishing operation and most of these publishers developed their lists themselves rather than through acquisition of small firms' assets.

The UK ELT publishers are especially adept at producing
tailor-made courses for particular countries or regions; and where
necessary (as in Asia), at producing courses in American English
sometimes via their own US-based ELT publishing arms. The
strategic importance of ELT is that it provides the publisher with
a local or regional foothold in non-English areas of the world
(such as Spain or the Far East, and potentially Eastern Europe),
either through the opening of local companies or marketing
offices or joint ventures with local publishers.

Academic, STM and professional book publishing

The internationalization through ownership of academic, STM
and professional book publishing occurred earlier than that of
consumer book publishing, and is far more extensive. High-level
books and journals, especially in STM, in the English language,
have an international currency, mainly throughout the developed
world. Such publishers rarely have to contend with literary
agents' retention of territorial rights and other rights. They
invariably acquire all rights in authors' works worldwide.

Again these fields are dominated by the large international
groups, plus the university presses and a range of independent
publishers. In the UK, the university press sector consists of
publishing divisions of universities (usually enjoying charitable
status, including the largest), commercial presses often with tenu-
ous links with their former universities (and branches of US
presses). Most UK presses, including the largest, act as commercial self-generating enterprises whereas in the USA the presses
are usually subsidized to a far greater degree. The US presses,
benefiting from the largest and richest home market and subsid-
ies issue large numbers of high-level research books at prices
which commercial US and UK publishers find difficult to match.
In the UK and within each main subject area, there are usually
around 15 to 20 publishers actively competing, and that includes
small independent UK publishers which specialize in particular
subjects or types of book.

The first stage in establishing a worldwide publishing network
involves opening sales and distribution offices or subsidiaries to

market imported books. Thus the larger US publishers opened offices in the UK and elsewhere, and UK publishers did the same in the US, but to a more limited extent, and elsewhere. Such offices then usually grew into publishing offices in their own right, feeding their originated books into the international network. Interestingly the largest UK university press has become the largest university press in America. The American STM giants and university presses quite often use their UK firms to handle international sales not only in Europe, but sometimes further afield. The US and UK publishers are exposed to competition and to take-overs from expansionist and large mainland European publishers, especially the Dutch and German which publish in English while mainland European publishers are exposed to US and UK take-overs.

In the world of international publishing, it is somewhat invidious to describe companies as US, UK, German or Dutch, other than on patriotic feelings. These majors are transnational in their approach to publishing. However, the location of the head office is significant.

As mentioned above, the UK publishers enjoyed heady growth in the 1960s and 1970s, but it slowed in the 1980s and UK sales in real terms fell after 1988 and flattened from 1989 through to 1991, as did title output. The fortunes of these publishers and the kinds of books they produce are inextricably linked to institutional spending on research, especially in relation to library budgets, to the numbers and wealth (or lack of it) of full-time and part-time students (particularly in UK higher education), and to the behaviour of librarians, researchers, teachers and students.

A major casualty of the virtually worldwide library cutbacks has been the publishing of high-priced academic hardback monographs, for so long a cornerstone of commercial academic publishing and of the university presses briefed to disseminate works of scholarship. For the scientists, the publication of research in a learned journal became more important than publication in the form of the monograph, whereas academics in the humanities and social sciences still needed to publish in full-length monograph. Throughout the 1980s selling just 1000 copies was progressively more difficult. Publishers reduced the costs of typesetting, and author royalty rates sometimes to zero, but even so, profitable publishing of potential monographs was increasingly problematic. By the turn of the decade academic libraries had moved from self-sufficiency in their collections to sharing copies through inter-library loans; and document suppliers copied individual chapters and journal articles for users, blighting book sales and subscriptions (see learned journals on p. 25).

A further difficulty affects the smaller UK publishers without a US publishing arm in common ownership. In order to access the important US library market, such UK publishers may enter into a co-publishing link with a US publisher, whereby the latter places a firm bulk quantity for a book and receives a high discount of, say, 70–85% off the UK published price. The US print order enables the UK publisher to spread the book's development costs (such as editing and typesetting) over the combined quantity thereby lowering the per copy cost and increasing its margin on its edition sold outside the USA.

On some books, a US order could be essential to the book's viability. The contract between them would exclude the US publisher from exporting copies but cannot preclude a third-party, such as a US exporting library supplier buying the books from the US publisher and exporting it overseas. Acquisition librarians in the major markets of northern Europe, Australia and the Pacific rim have bibliographic databases listing the prices of the US and UK editions of the same book. If the US edition is significantly cheaper and there is a US exporting supplier offering them a discount off that lower price, they will order the US edition, other factors being equal. Thus the UK publisher would find copies supplied to its US partner at a very high discount entering markets to which it expected to sell its own edition profitability at lower discounts. It is estimated that about one-third of UK academic library expenditure is spent on books directly imported into the UK mainly by UK branches of US publishers, but a few imports might by UK-originated books making a round trip from America.

The 'buying around' by third-parties of the territorial contractual arrangements made between publishers is not restricted to high-priced academic, STM and professional books destined for libraries. American exporting wholesalers and remainder dealers supply US editions of UK-originated trade books to retailers in Europe and elsewhere. International ownership of publishers and of IPR in titles allows a publisher to control pricing in markets throughout the world.

In the context of academic monograph publishing, the commercial publishers drastically pruned their lists and some of the university presses persevered with a more limited range. The publishers and presses switched their attention to producing greater numbers of supplementary textbooks and titles of professional interest, published in paperback at lower prices, for the high-level undergraduate, optional courses, and for professional training or practitioner areas such as in management, teacher training, and health and social welfare. While high-priced research or reference books usually have a wide international readership, textbooks are increasingly developed for, or adapted to, UK and north European markets, though these can (more so in the STM fields) be exported to the USA, Australia and the Pacific rim.

UK undergraduate students are poor, may share books (less so in some science fields) and their teachers may develop their own bespoke courses consisting of photocopied extracts from books and journals. In the USA, the second-hand textbook market is so developed that sales of a new book fall fast after the first year of publication, whereas in the UK the sales of a good textbook will increase. From the start of the 1990s, UK student numbers increased dramatically as did those of mature (post-21) students who are better book buyers. Book sales did not match the growth in student numbers but nonetheless publisher's title output rose again, as did sales and profitability.

Learned journals

Journal publishing, especially in STM, has been immensely profitable. Academic libraries, under stress during the 1980s, generally tried to maintain their STM journal collections at the expense of book purchases. However, continued worldwide library cutbacks in the early 1990s and increased journal prices led to order cancellations of the weaker journals and cramped the growth of new journals. Moreover, the acquisition policies of libraries have increasingly switched from that of self-sufficiency in collections to that of co-operation between libraries, through the use of inter-library loans and of remote document (e.g. journal article) supply. Overseas, particularly in the USA, there are commercial document suppliers offering current awareness services which summarize the contents pages of journals and monographs, and transmit via the network the relevant article or chapter to users. In the UK, statutory exceptions permit non-profit libraries to offer copies for research and private study on a royalty free basis. The British Library Document Supply Centre at Boston Spa, using this exception and its stock of over seven million books, journals and theses, dominates the document supply, photocopying market to over 14 000 regular clients in academia, government and business. From a user's viewpoint it offers an excellent service; from a publisher's or commercial document supplier's viewpoint it is a cause of friction – though its new services such as electronic document supply and photo-copying outside the statutory exception, may come under new payment arrangements.

The developments of electronic networks, especially in academia, and of electro-copying enable users in an organization connected to a Local Area Network (LAN) or Wide Area Network (WAN), to log in and view, download and transfer the full text of relevant articles. Furthermore, the networks allow article writers to communicate them directly to other readers; and some academic institutions and societies, and publishers have developed embryo electronic journals. The self-electronic publishing by writers themselves without charge can proliferate the numbers of junk articles as refereeing standards are unclear.

At first sight such developments could conceivably be the death-knell of printed journals and of the publishers which dominate the research information supply business. But there are good reasons for the continuance of printed journals and of publishers. Printed journals still enjoy greater peer group respect, the reward factor to authors of appearing in print rather than merely on a VDU is greater, and paper as a medium is more satisfying for some people to recall and easier to browse through. While electronic journals are seemingly easier and cheaper to produce (no engagement with printers) and faster to disseminate (no physical distribution), they still need copy-editing, the text requires coding to ensure that presentation, bibliographic and archiving standards are maintained, and they need management, marketing and the collection of money. The existing publishers own the established paper-based journals and are the main creators of new ones. Worldwide journal publishing is their core business, for an individual academic institution it is not. Once payment systems are in place, and international agreements are reached on presentation and formatting standards, it is expected that paid-for electronic journals and their revenues will grow, as will document supply, at the expense of paper-based journal subscriptions. Quite possibly, electronic versions will be available in parallel with printed ones, for instance the electronic version could be transmitted to subscribers in advance and complete sets of journals could be released on CD-ROM.

MIXED MEDIA, MULTIMEDIA AND NETWORK PUBLISHING

The book and learned journal publishers derive by far their largest turnover and profits from the supply of print-based products.

Mixed media publishing

Some major publishers are part of media corporations in the sense that such organizations may consist of generally free-standing divisions encompassing, for example, newspapers, magazines, books and television companies etc. The book publishers in general, however, engage in publishing of non-print products to a very limited extent. Examples include the publishing of audiobooks (typically abridged mass-market fiction on two C90 cassettes, about 30 000 words of reading over three hours) as freestanding items; or of mixed media packs (usually book and audiocassette) in children's publishing or for early reading, and for foreign language learning (occasionally supplemented with videocassette). The educational and ELT publishers publish audiocassettes and sometimes videocassettes for teachers who have adopted the publisher's books to use in class. Some science, technology and computing college textbooks, especially imports from the USA, may have floppy disks attached. In professional fields, a few publishers have divisions concerned with business and management training and they produce mixed media self-learning packs. Generally speaking the non-book products are added-value items to the books themselves, used to enhance the scope of the printed word (such as in language learning) or to aid textbook adoptions.

Multimedia publishing

The emergence of a number of new technologies facilitates the development of interactive multimedia products (i.e. the integration of text, sound and of images, both moving and still, within a single digital environment) and that might be on an optical storage compact disc, such as CD-ROM (Compact Disc Read Only Memory) and its derivatives, or on a memory card for a hand-held computer – applications sometimes referred to as electronic books. Competing hardware and software companies are developing different, sometimes incompatible systems, and each needs products or applications on which to sell their systems. In some cases they will finance publishers or multimedia producers to develop products. On the other hand, publishers and multimedia producers may be reluctant to commit themselves to a particular system or platform which may turn out to be a failure.

Compact disc (CD) technologies are arousing the greatest interest and speculation. CDs, or 'silver discs', have affinities with books in that they are intellectual physical products (more robust than floppy disks) which can be traded like books directly to end-users by mail or via retailers. A CD-ROM disc has a large storage capacity (about 250 000 pages of text alone, say 200 average length books) and more recently, can incorporate sound, reasonably high-quality photographs, animated graphics and full-motion video. Advocates stress such added media dimensions and trumpet the word 'interactive'. They play down the current difficulties of easily browsing through the material; and of reading linear text, stories or arguments on screen which can be tiring and tends to be less reflective than reading from a book.

The first multimedia products available on CD included those of a structured reference nature (existing copyright in which is solely or mainly held by the book publisher) such as dictionaries, encyclopaedias, almanacs, and highly-illustrated information titles; do-it-yourself manuals with added realism and application; children's picture books transformed into interactive story books; illustrated derivatives from children's television series and educational reference titles for schools; and multi-language teaching applications. Many CD-ROM titles are text databases (i.e. a large body of information made up of individual items held in a form which enables users to locate, correlate and retrieve items as required; for example, bibliographies) for professional use, produced for narrow and specialist markets needing little multimedia interactivity, the copyright in which is usually held by publishers.

Electronic titles are produced by new divisions of book or magazine publishers alone or in joint ventures with others such as multimedia producers (or packagers) or software and hardware manufacturers, and by media corporations, or by new dedicated companies. Interactive multimedia needs the combination of illustrated book editorial, design and graphic skills with that of sound producers and of television producers or editors who understand the importance of pace, timing and emotion. Furthermore, ease of use by purchasers depends greatly on the underlying software and interface design skills of the programmers. The development costs are thus usually very high in comparison to books yet published prices of some CDs are dropping to the levels of their printed equivalents. In addition, clearing copyright permissions with third-parties such as film, video, sound and photographic libraries and other publishers who believe they are about to reap immediate new fortunes can be arduous and expensive.

Producing, marketing and selling multimedia products is a high-risk venture. The take-up of players is growing but still limited. However, the stakes are enormous for the hardware manufacturers which are driving the market forward. The computer industry's slowing growth and falling margins from traditional corporate markets stimulate the development of more user-friendly computers with more useful multimedia applications for the home and for education. It is expected that CD-ROM drives will be standard built-in features on most personal computers (PCs). In the USA, the installed domestic base of powerful PCs with CD-ROM drives is large and fast expanding. In the UK it is comparatively small, though UK school computers for example, are equipped with CD-ROM drives, as in the universities. At the same time, the major consumer electronics companies and games companies are developing their own multimedia platforms, designed as domestic appliances based on the television rather than on the computer, and more for entertainment than for studious education and work.

The first wave of selling consumer multimedia titles was by way of mail-order catalogues to enthusiasts or as complimentary items with hardware. However, such products like their book counterparts need retail exposure. UK retailers stocking multimedia include computer stores, video chains and music shops. In the USA some bookshops stock them and it is argued that bookshops should be their natural home. CDs present special difficulties in achieving distinctive retail packaging and need demonstration at the point-of-sale or at exhibitions, such as by trained sales staff or through trial at home or workplace. In the latter, a publisher might for instance give a potential purchaser a taster of the disc's contents, or subsequent access to its other contents through the provision of codes supplied on receipt of the purchaser's money. Like successful books, electronic titles need regular changes to the design and content in order to keep on selling. Some publishers are beginning to employ electronic product managers who may be drawn from the audio, video and software industries.

Network publishing

The convergence of technologies, or seemingly separate industries such as telecom, satellite and cable TV companies, and leisure and information providers, through the potential of land-based cable networks is capturing the imagination of technological pundits, social commentators, multinational corporations, investors and the banks. The transmission capability of picture, voice and data via satellite or terrestrial stations through the air is more limited than that of land-based cable networks, especially if fibre optic.

Since at least the early 1970s commercial on-line databases have been available. They normally engage the information provider, the database host (providing the central computer holding a variety of databases and managing on-line access to customers) and the network operator (usually a telecom company). Overwhelmingly such on-line databases provide high-value, fast changing real-time financial information for the world's equity, commodity and currency markets. In respect of the book publishing industry, its use has been slight. The real-time cost to users, especially the high network tariffs charged by the former telecom monopoly, has proved very expensive in relation to the purchase of reference books, even for lawyers.

In the early 1970s, a US Department of Defense network project established Internet, eventually taken over by academia under a public service ethos to allow free and unrestricted movement of information. It subsequently crossed the Atlantic, and now comprises thousands of connected networks forming the basis of a 'global information superhighway'. Meanwhile in the UK, a collaboration between the universities created the Joint Academic Network (JANET) which links up academics' and libraries' computers. Its planned successor, SuperJANET is a highspeed optical fibre network allowing the interchange at low cost of high-quality data, such as text, graphics and video throughout higher education. Academics initially used such connected networks for document transfer and electronic mail (E-mail) between themselves on and off the campus, in north America, Europe and elsewhere. From an academic's viewpoint the service appeared free and convenient. By the early 1990s the more alert academic and STM publishers became connected in order to communicate electronically with their authors.

In the 1980s, Internet was the playground of academics; now it is developing considerable commercial potential. The use by commerce and industry of Internet is outstripping that of academia, and allows the more advanced publishers, document suppliers and booksellers to market and sell products directly. City analysts who already rate STM and professional book and journal publishers higher than those in the consumer field, envisage further earnings growth stemming from the added value the networks will give to their products.

Printed books and journals are freestanding objects and are seemingly 'offline', as are CDs. But electrocopying allows printed documents to be scanned, digitized, stored in computers, searched, manipulated and transmitted via networks; and multimedia CDs are already digital. Once put on a network, they become 'online' and vulnerable to worldwide copyright infringement and plagiarism. Librarians and academic computing departments add value for their users through networking resources. For publishers and authors the various ways of the licensing of copyright works for networking and payment systems are unclear. (CD-ROMs for professional reference and networking tend to be licensed rather than sold outright and can include security systems against improper use.) Nevertheless once copyright payment and security systems are fully in place the opportunities for publishers to provide information and teaching materials on CD or online or by document delivery are greatly enhanced.

The linkage of such networks via the telephone network helps academics and others (including publishers' editors) to work from home and to communicate easily with the campus, office and other people so connected. However, the prospects that the capacity of existing cables will be upgraded with optical fibre, and that other cable network providers would in due course install optical fibre cables to people's homes, offer greater scope for interactive television and home shopping, leisure and information provision, and potentially lower network tariffs as the networks compete for business. The network providers might be telecom and cable television companies or others. The potential and enormous value of such networks encourages the banks in the USA and UK to finance their installation. Moreover, in the so-called information age the companies (such as film, television, music and print) which hold IPR – the information content – are perceived in vague terms to have enhanced value and are attractive for investment or as take-over targets by computer and software companies, by consumer electronic and network companies etc. In the context of book publishing, it should be noted that the copyright in illustrations is often owned by others; that many of the old contracts signed with authors did not include electronic publishing rights thus such rights reside with authors; that in more recent publishing contracts, authors grant publishers electronic rights; but that in the consumer field, literary agents will often try to retain electronic rights unless they can be persuaded by a book publisher to grant them.

Every technological breakthrough such as the introduction of television, and the quite widespread deployment of PCs in the early 1980s, has always been accompanied by pundits within and outside book publishing foretelling the demise of the book. Nevertheless on a worldwide basis, book publishing has grown apace, and for the foreseeable future most book publishers are optimistic. Books and electronic titles are mutually compatible not diametrically opposed. In some fields electronic titles provide better ways of communicating information, in others books are superior, while in others books and electronic titles may be used together. Low-cost networks into people's homes might provide a wider distribution channel than conventional hard-copy book trade channels. The developing electronic media markets open up new channels and formats for authors and publishers to exploit.

2

Sectors of publishing

Although there are common themes in all book publishing there are marked differences in the ways different kinds of books are published for different markets. Publishers specialize in reaching particular markets. The skills of their staff, the activities they perform and the structure of the business are aligned accordingly.

All kinds of publishers can be described as serving niche markets. Attaining a critical mass in a particular field, right down to a list of books on the narrowest subject area, is vital to publishers of every size. It allows the employment of editors who understand and have contact with authors and associates in a particular field, and who can shape projects for their intended markets. A respected list attracts authors. Furthermore, a list of books needs to generate sufficient turnover to allow effective and focused marketing and selling which in turn feeds new publishing. At the broadest level, the main sectors of publishing are as follows.

CONSUMER BOOK PUBLISHING

The consumer book publishers (sometimes called 'trade' or 'general' publishers) are the most visible part of the industry. Their adult and children's fiction and non-fiction hardback and paperback titles are displayed prominently in high street bookshops and other outlets, receive considerable mass-media coverage and are aimed mainly at the indefinable 'general reader', sometimes at the enthusiast or specialist reader. They form (in hardback though increasingly in paperback) the mainstay of public libraries and book clubs, and in some cases penetrate the student/academic markets. Such books account for about 57% of the industry's sales value, and about 21% are exported. The most active UK book buyers tend to be female, the 25–44 age group, the better-off social classes, and located in the south rather than the north. While about 20% of book sales are made to the highly educated, often metropolitan, AB social grades, 80% of new paperback buyers and 78% of new hardback buyers come from the C1/C2/DE socio-economic grades.

Most publishers (including the majors and most medium-sized independent firms) are in London giving them ready access to authors, authors' agents, other publishers, social venues, journalists and producers of the mass-media, and other influential people who decisively affect the life of the nation. The remaining publishers are spread around the country, in Scotland, and tend to be more specialized.

Consumer book publishing is the high-risk end of the business: book failures are frequent but the possible rewards from 'bestsellers' – some of which are quite unexpected – are great. The potential readers are varied, spread very thinly through the population, expensive to reach, difficult to identify and to locate, and have tastes and interests that can be described generally but are not easily matched to a particular book. These publishers bet to a great extent on their judgement of public taste and interests – notoriously unpredictable. Sometimes the publication of a book creates its own market. And the authors whose work arouses growing interest can develop a personal readership, thereby creating their own markets – perhaps attaining a 'brand name' following, especially in fiction. Publishers compete fiercely for their books.

Publishers are opportunistic – they must respond fast if they want to capture a well known author or personality, or take advantage of current fashions, media events or topical issues on which to hang a book's promotion. Additionally, some firms want to fulfil the traditional role of publishing literary works, and of developing authors who may in the future be recognized as having written a great work. But only a few authors and books become part of the eternal backlist. The public libraries still underpin to some extent the hardback publishing of some serious fiction and non-fiction, and there are novelists who are heavily borrowed but not bought.

Few other consumer goods industries market products with such a short sales life. Generally speaking for a book's sales life to survive, it is vital for the publisher to secure advance pre-publication 'subscription' orders from booksellers and for the response to the book to be good in the opening weeks post-publication. The peak sales of most new books occur within a year of publication. Most adult hardback fiction and paperback titles are dead within three months or just weeks, while hardback non-fiction and paperback fiction written by famous authors may endure longer. Most houses earn more than half their revenue from the new books (frontlist). Some publishers are very frontlist weighted, while others keep strong backlists alive from their new book programme and by relaunching old books in new covers, re-issuing them in different sizes and bindings, adding new introductions or revising them. An energetically promoted backlist provides retailers with staple and more predictable stock, should earn good profits for the publisher, and keeps authors in print.

Many readers mistakenly believe that the large price differential between hardbacks and paperbacks is due to the extra cost of binding a book in hardback. The considerable price gap does not represent that cost (which is low): rather it often reflects aggregate print runs, revealing the economics of product differentiation by which publishers try to satisfy different expectations and demands of public and institutional purchasers. The binding styles and paperback sizes (A, B and C formats) are symbolic of the markets. For example, a fiction title could be launched first in hardback at a high price to satisfy eager readers, libraries and sometimes a book club then subsequently at a lower price to reach a new and wider market of readers in trade or mass-market paperback; or it might be originally published in trade paperback. Furthermore many titles of minority appeal could not recover their investment if first published in a lower paperback price range established for books with higher sales potential over which the costs could be spread.

In comparison with other publishers consumer book publishers tend to operate in the following ways:

- They pay a half to two-thirds or more of what they expect the author to earn from royalties from sales of the first printing – paid in instalments (e.g. on signature of contract between author and publisher, on delivery or acceptance of manuscript, on publication).
- They tend to give much greater emphasis to their top authors in terms of promotional expenditure, sales effort and publi-

cation dates to maximize sales. However, it is possible for them to gain great free media coverage on other books.

- They depend to a far greater extent on retail exposure to sell their books, and on gift buying of adult and children's books (the pre-Christmas period is of immense importance); but they suffer from greater returns of unsold books from retailers and wholesalers (around 20% of sales). While their main customers are the bookselling chains, these publishers have a wide range of other retail, wholesale, and book club distribution channels available to them. The choice of books by centralized buyers of retail chains and of wholesalers determined to satisfy their differing customer profiles inevitably influences publishers.

- They have greater scope to sell rights in the author's work to other firms, and to set up co-edition deals with others (e.g. book clubs, overseas publishers etc.). The co-printing of two or more editions together allows the originator to spread high development and printing costs (especially on highly illustrated adult and children's colour books) over several markets, thereby making the book affordable to the readers in each market. Adult and children's publishers specializing in books which sell on the strength of the illustrations (including art book publishers) make great use of this technique.

Some publishers producing mass-market low-priced illustrated hardbacks and paperbacks sometimes pre-sell bulk quantities of own-brand books to large retailers, thereby obviating risk.

Children's publishing

Children's books are published by the specialist children's divisions of the major consumer book publishers with both hardback and paperback lists, independent children's book publishers and by the major university press. The vitality of children's publishing creates the book buyers of the future. As on the adult side, there are a number of book packagers creating books for publishers, typically on an international co-edition basis.

An unusual feature of children's publishing is that although the text and illustrations of these books must excite and appeal to children of different age groups, at different levels of reading skill and comprehension, they must also appeal to adults in the supply chain (the major non-book and book retailers, wholesalers, book clubs) and to adults who buy or influence choice (such as parents, relations, librarians and teachers). Furthermore, in that many titles include much colour yet have to be published at low prices, such titles often need co-edition partners in the USA, in Europe and elsewhere in order to attain economies in printing.

The books are usually aimed at age bands reflecting the development of reading skill. The 0–5 age group from babies to toddlers may be described as the parent pointing stage. Included here are the so-called 'novelty books' (which extend above the age group), a category of book of ever-widening inventiveness, such as board books and bath books (introducing page turning), sound story books with electronic panels, colouring and activity books, question and answer books, pop-ups etc.; and the lower end of picture books. Books for the very young need to be very durable and often use cloth, plastic or hardback binding.

The 5–8 age group may be described as the starting to read, as well as reading to children stage. Picture books figure prominently. These books, invariably in full colour, tend to be 32 pages long (12–14 double-page spreads), display strong narrative and may include just a few words up to possibly several thousand; they may be created by an illustrator or writer (or one controlling mind), and invariably need co-edition partners. Story books for younger fiction tend to have more text, say 2000–7500 words and may be published in paperback in smaller formats, with black and white, or colour illustrations; and are designed for children reading their first whole novels. There are major series produced by many of the main publishers. Moving up, and through, the 9–12 age group, longer length novels of up to 40 000 words come into play as well as the more recent mass-market genre series. Above 11–12, there are the teenage or young adult, fiction titles.

Non-fiction, sometimes highly illustrated, spans the age groups as do home learning series, reference titles (e.g. dictionaries), anthologies and character books (some which are tie-ins to films etc.) and so on.

Broadly speaking, in comparison with adult consumer book publishers, authors' advances tend to be lower (reflecting the lower published prices); and children's publishers of quality books earn a higher proportion from backlist sales – the thirst for established favourites is constantly assuaged.

Children's publishing in the UK continues to push out the frontiers of book availability into a wide range of retail outlets, including grocery, toy and garden centres etc. reached directly, or indirectly via wholesalers. Such retailers, and some of the book clubs, tend to concentrate on books for the younger age groups. Internationally, the Bologna Book Fair held in the spring is the world's meeting place of children's publishing. The UK publishers and packagers have for long dominated the international trade in the selling of overseas co-edition rights though, like their adult counterparts, they import far less.

Consumer mail-order publishers

A few publishers sell enormous quantities of books to readers predominantly by mail order: retail sales are additional. Examples of their output include condensed fiction, and highly illustrated information titles (including atlases, dictionaries and other reference titles) published individually, or in series, for UK households and, where appropriate, abroad. Their strengths lie in their mailing lists containing discriminative information on millions of households, their expertise in selling by mail order and (on information titles especially) their use of the mailing lists for scientific market research on projects before publication (e.g. the testing of concepts, content, price etc.) and their development of complex books to suit the market.

Promotional book publishers

Bargain books (sometimes referred to as 'manufactured remainders' or 'promotion books') are primarily aimed at the gift buyer, like so many consumer books; but more specifically not so much at the hardcore regular book buyers frequenting bookshops but at the great majority of people thinking of buying something of enduring value keenly priced and on impulse. The nature and low price of these books compete head on against other gift choices. Bargain hardbacks and paperbacks are usually mainstream, slow-dating non-fiction preferably international subjects such as cookery, gardening, do-it-yourself, children's reference, leisure, hobbies and art though contemporary fiction is also available.

Bargain books, some of which are reprints of successful remainders (e.g. overstocks of publishers' full-priced editions sold off cheaply to clear warehouse space), are produced by promotional book publishers, an American term denoting promotional on price, low retail price, not through sponsorship. Such publishers can be in part remainder dealers; or they are predominantly concerned with reprinting, repackaging or originating material. They may be independently owned with their own specialities, or are divisions of the major consumer book publishers drawing on their former hardback and paperback full-priced editions. Promotional publishers may repackage material in book form which first appeared in magazines or in part works, scour through publishers' lists of suitable out-of-print books, find out-of-copyright works, or originate new bargain books themselves, or commission book packagers to produce books for them. Payments to authors, if any, have to be minimized through one-off fees. These books must offer overt perceived value for money – big and chunky, bulked up on thick paper if necessary, with lots of colour and powerful, straightforward non-intimidating jackets or covers. In order to achieve very low prices the books must be printed in large quantities, say more than 20 000 copies. A promotional house sells them to the UK bargain chains and bookshops, to UK direct selling operations, and pre-sells large English language firm orders to promotional houses abroad (e.g. in the USA, Australia, South Africa, New Zealand, Canada) which sell to their own bargain chains etc.; to overseas trade publishers if possible at higher prices; and to foreign language publishers, on an international co-edition basis.

NON-CONSUMER BOOK PUBLISHING

The educational, academic, scientific, technical and medical (STM), and professional book publishers (accounting for about a third of the industry's sales) have a great advantage in that:

- the markets for which they publish are more defined;
- their authors and advisers are drawn mainly from the same peer groups as the readers who strongly influence the choice of books bought;
- these groups can be reached through their place of work.

Educational publishing

The educational publishers provide materials for schools: chiefly textbooks bought in multiple copies, sometimes supported by ancillary printed materials for class use or for teachers (and where appropriate audiocassettes, atlases, software, CD-ROM etc.), published individually or as a series (e.g. representing a progressive course of study). Publishers concentrate on the big subject areas. School publications represent about 9% of home market sales value. Not many educational publishers are in central London, most are located in cheaper locations such as the New Town ring, Oxford and Cambridge.

The books are market-specific (i.e. precisely tailored to the National Curriculum, examinations, academic levels and age groups). While to some extent the broad content is pre-determined, publishers with their external advisers and authors give great attention to the pedagogy, influence curriculum development, and also cater for more conservative teachers. They help raise the quality of teaching. Many books are highly illustrated, increasingly printed in colour, and involve a publisher in much development work. Yet they must be published at very low prices. Book provision in state schools is always under-funded.

Compared with consumer book publishing, educational publishing is long-term. Most publishers derive most of their sales revenue from established backlist books. Schools can ill afford to dump adopted texts frequently. New books are published in the hope that they will be reprinted and revised in following years, but in practice may fail. Educational publishing calls for a large amount of working capital invested over a long time. These features make life very difficult for small publishers or those wanting to enter the field.

New and backlist titles are promoted by mail directly to teachers and by publishers' sales representatives in schools and at exhibitions. Teachers scrutinize bound copies before adopting a book. Textbooks are supplied directly to schools or via booksellers, specialist school contractors and local authority direct purchasing organizations, and may be stocked by booksellers for parental purchase.

Some educational publishers produce books for further education (especially for vocational qualifications), self-education, reference, and exam revision aids which are sold through bookshops.

UK-orientated school textbooks generally have drastically reduced export potential though there can be scope, for example, to produce specially prepared textbooks, such as in science and mathematics, for poor countries dependent on aid agency funding.

In contrast, the publishing of English Language Teaching (ELT) or English as a Foreign Language (EFL) course materials is export-orientated (say above 90% of sales) to better-off countries and has to some extent offset the overall decline in exports of UK school books. The main markets, in addition to the UK, are Europe (Spain, Greece, Italy, France, Turkey), Japan, the Far East and South East Asia (Hong Kong, Taiwan, Korea, Thailand), Latin America (Argentina, Brazil and Mexico) and the Middle East intermittently. The ELT publishers have set up companies or opened offices or acquired publishers in such areas, or have co-publishing links with local publishers, or local marketing arrangements.

The mixed media ELT courses are major investments and may be orientated or versioned to regional cultural distinctiveness and are sometimes produced for ministries. The courses serving primary, secondary and adult sectors are backed up with supplementary materials (such as reading books, dictionaries and grammars) with a broad international appeal. They are sold to the Private Language Schools (PLS) (from primary to adult), primary and secondary state schools, sometimes to universities. In the UK there are specialist booksellers supplying the local and export markets.

Academic, STM and professional book publishing

The publishing of high-level school books may cross over to college courses. Academic publishing can refer to books published in all subjects from first-year university/college students and above, but the term is sometimes restricted to the humanities and social sciences alone in which some imprints of large publishers, or smaller independent publishers, specialize. Scientific, technical and medical (STM) publishing is a relatively distinct area undertaken especially by large publishers. UK academic and STM publishers associated with US firms import numerous US originated titles.

These publishers are mostly outside central London with a high concentration in Oxford, and their output (representing about 29% of the industry's sales) includes first-year introductory textbooks (mainly the preserve of larger publishers); higher level supplementary textbooks for more advanced students through to postgraduate; edited volumes of reprinted or commissioned articles for students or academics; research monographs; books for professional use; reference titles (some on CD-ROM) and learned journals. These broad categories are not clear cut (e.g. high-level 'textbooks' may incorporate original research).

Broadly speaking textbooks are published in paperback, though some for professional training (e.g. medicine, law) may be hardback. The high-level textbooks occasionally have a short high-priced print run for libraries, issued simultaneously with the paperback. Monographs are usually short-lived high-priced hardbacks published mainly for libraries and to a far less extent for personal purchase, and are printed in small quantities (e.g. 500–750 copies) once only, though a few are re-issued in paper-back (monographs are a speciality of the major university presses). Short-run publishing is not risk free – the profit may come from the sale of the last fifty copies. Conversely, textbooks, printed in larger quantities, may become established and are reprinted for annual student intakes and revised through new editions. Competitors constantly attack the market share of successful books. The successful sale of a textbook entails persuading the lecturer to adopt it, the bookseller to stock it and the student to buy it. Many of the bookshops are owned by the bookselling chains. Nevertheless, publishers have been more successful than the consumer book publishers in resisting booksellers' demands for higher discounts, and in containing author royalty rates, and advances if any. Trade wholesalers find it difficult to enter the supply chain. Returns of unsold books are around 12%.

These publishers promote (and sometimes sell directly) their books to lecturers, researchers and practitioners (mainly by mail and telephone) and compared with consumer book publishers usually have smaller sales forces calling on a limited range of booksellers. However, some firms publish titles of wider general interest and of bookshop appeal in which case booksellers may be granted higher 'trade' discounts. These include more titles in the humanities than the social sciences, some technical books (e.g. on computing) and medical works (e.g. personal health). They are sometimes bought by general book clubs.

Not even the largest publisher could claim to be equally strong in all disciplines, or even those in science alone. Publishers concentrate on particular subjects, and vary in the emphasis given to different categories of book.

The high-priced books for professional or practitioner use which have a wider market beyond teaching institutions, tend to be those in the applied sciences for researchers or practitioners in industry and government agencies; and those serving professional sectors (e.g. law, medicine, management, accounting, finance, architecture). Such titles are bought by the wealthy (offices, commercial libraries and individuals). Special sales channels include training companies serving corporations, agencies and individuals; dedicated business, computer and medical book distributors or book clubs reaching end-users directly; conference and exhibition organizers; and companies which take bulk orders of titles as promotional items.

The legal and financial publishers, especially, use loose-leaf publishing for some of their reference titles. The purchaser, having bought the initial volume, receives updated pages at intervals on a standing order. However, some major reference works are completely updated regularly and supplied on standing order. Such publishers, as well as those producing books for business, sell a high proportion of their materials by mail order to end-users, not via booksellers. Sometimes, reference books (including directories) are written in-house. They may supply the information via electronic means (e.g. via on-line database hosts if time-sensitive valuable data, or on CD-ROM).

Typically over 50% of the output of these publishers is exported. (It accounts for about a third of the total of all books exported.) As English is the world's scientific language, STM publications are often more exportable.

Western Europe and North America account for about 50% of export sales, followed by the Far East and Southeast Asia, and Australia. For many publishers, mainland Europe is the single most important market but one which is diverse and growing. The Scandinavian and Benelux countries can be significant markets for English language textbook adoptions, and for professional lists. Holland in terms of sales often ranks third after the USA and Australia, and is dominated by a few major bookselling chains, while Germany, another large market, is served by a variety of regional and local chains. Southern Europe, such as Spain and Italy, is a market for high-level professional texts, especially in STM; undergraduate texts exist in translation or are published locally.

High-level textbooks and professional titles are sold to the USA, the largest and richest market, via the UK publisher's US counterpart. A UK firm without a US presence may develop a co-publishing link with a US firm, or license rights to a variety of publishers, or sell through importers.

Sales to poor countries tend to be dependent on aid agency funding. Publishers may produce special low-priced editions of textbooks, sometimes facilitated by the UK government through subsidy.

Journal publishing

The content of learned journals, as distinct from magazines, is not predetermined (commissioned or written in-house), rather contributors submit papers of original research to an academic editor for refereeing and inclusion. As such, refereed journal articles are a primary information source, establish or enhance academic standing of authors (counting towards their research funding and their promotion prospects), and serve the research community. Generally speaking, learned journals are not dependent on advertising for their viability; their revenue is derived mostly from subscriptions.

Journals are published by societies and research institutes (a few of which run substantial journal and book publishing operations), and by divisions of academic and STM publishers including the university presses. The latter initiate journals, or produce and market journals for societies and others.

The key people in a journal publisher are the commissioning editors who bring in new journals, the production editors who organize and produce them, direct mail specialists who market them directly to academia etc., and subscription service specialists; plus, where appropriate, advertising sales staff.

There are more STM journals than academic, and nearly two-thirds of sales are exports. Many journals are printed in the

500–3000 copy range. They are promoted by mail, supplied on subscription, sold mainly to academic libraries worldwide (often via subscription agents) and to a lesser extent sold direct to individuals (more so in the USA). Journals of applied science, management, economics and law also sell to industrial and commercial libraries. (Members of societies may receive a journal free as part of their membership fee, or at a reduced rate.) Journal academic editors may be paid, but contributors and referees are not. Limited offprints are usually supplied to authors for their private distribution.

The great advantage is that annual subscriptions are received in advance of production and can be used for other acquisitions. But new journals take a long time to break even (e.g. more than five years for some STM journals). Once established, the sales pattern is more predictable than books, the demand for capital is lower (as are staff overheads), and the value of sales per employee is higher.

Journal publishing, unlike book publishing, does not require a sales force or a complex network of overseas agents. The discounts granted to subscription agents may be from 0 to 10%. The credit risk is low, and the return of unsolds rare. Other income can arise from advertisements and inserts (especially in STM), from sales of back issues and of additional offprints, from copyright fees from commercial document suppliers and from subscription list rental. The lists and journals can be used to advertise and sell the publisher's books. There is cross-fertilization of contacts and ideas between book and journal publishers. However continued worldwide library cutbacks and the rise in document supply of individual articles, falling volumes of subscriptions and of revenues despite price increases, combined with lower costs, speed of delivery and potentially lower prices of electronic journals which might allow new entrepreneurial firms to enter the field, pose considerable challenges to the existing commercial and non-profit publishers alike.

Reference publishing

Reference works (spanning words, pictures, numbers, maps etc.) are sold by all kinds of publisher from consumer book to professional. Although some are ephemeral, reference publishing is usually for the long-term backlist. Major works (such as dictionaries) can take years to compile and can involve investments of millions.

Reference publishing is most amenable to the application of new technologies in terms of aiding the product development and the publishing of a family of products in different media (e.g. on paper and/or on CD-ROM), of different sizes and prices for various markets. For example, in dictionary publishing the lexicographers (and in bilingual works, translators) no longer have to rely on the manual identification and retrieval of words in primary sources. Typically they use electronic text corpora holding a vast range of primary and diverse sources from which evidence of word meaning and sentence contextual meaning can be retrieved, manipulated and to an increasing extent analysed electronically. Once the main dictionary database has been built and coded, spin-off shorter or special purpose dictionaries can be subsequently published. Atlas and cartographic publishers have traditionally faced the problem that survey information is usually held by other parties. However, they are now able to purchase satellite information from which they can build and update their own cartographic databases.

3

From author contract to market outlet

This chapter opens with a review of the importance of copyright to authors and publishers, and gives an example of the contractual relationship between them. In that literary agents represent many of the professional writers of fiction and non-fiction books, agents' work is described, and the ways in which it may affect the scope of the publisher to sell the author's work in various forms worldwide are covered. Also included here is the role of book packagers, an important source of highly illustrated books for some publishers. Most publishers do not sell books directly to readers. Publishers' main customers are thus the booksellers and other intermediaries. The ever-widening channels of distribution in the UK book trade market are outlined in the last section, together with the debate on the Net Book Agreement.

COPYRIGHT

Book publishing today rests on copyright. In general terms, copyright is a form of protection, giving authors and other creative artists legal proprietorship (ownership) of their work – that is, it establishes their work as their personal, exclusive property; and because it is their property they have the absolute right to sell or license it to others, or not.

It is these exclusive rights that make author's works attractive to publishers. What the publisher wants from authors is the sole, exclusive right to publish their work and sell it as widely as possible. Without the protection of copyright, authors would not be able to grant this exclusive right and could not demand payment for their efforts; and publishers would not risk issuing a book which, if successful, could be instantly copied or plundered by competitors. Copyright stimulates innovation and protects the author's reputation.

For copyright to subsist in a literary work (one which is written, spoken or sung) it must be 'original' (i.e. some effort, skill or judgement needs to have been exercised to attract copyright protection) and it must be recorded in writing or otherwise. There is no copyright in ideas: copyright exists in the concrete form of expression, the arrangement of the words.

Copyright protection endures for the author's life plus fifty years from the year end of the author's death. After that period the work enters the public domain. Publishers compete fiercely on the pricing of public domain classics on which no royalties need be paid.

Through the European Commission (EC) authors' statutory rights are strengthening and include the moral rights of **paternity** (the author's right to be credited as the author of the work) and of **integrity** (the author's right to be protected from editorial distortion of the work). Such moral rights are likely to grow in importance in the age of electronic publications which frequently involve substantial adaptation of authors' and illustrators' work, greatly ease the manipulation of authors' works and facilitate the risks of non-attribution and of plagiarism. The EC also intends to harmonize copyright duration, up to seventy years from the author's death, as in Germany, to take effect on 1st July, 1995.

Works created by employees in working hours (and covered, as a further safeguard, by their terms and conditions of service) are the copyright of the employer. Publishers who commission freelance editors, technical illustrators, indexers and software engineers ensure that copyright is assigned in writing to the publisher through an agreement. The publisher's typographical layout of the page is the copyright of the publisher and that lasts for twenty-five years from publication. Copyright exists in compilations, such as databases, provided that there is an adequate degree of originality in the selection and arrangement of the information.

AUTHOR–PUBLISHER CONTRACTS

Each publisher draws up its own contract (or agreement) and each contract differs with the book and the author. Commissioning editors negotiate contracts with authors or their agents. The contract defines formally and in detail the relationship between author and publisher.

Items covered in a typical contract between author and publisher

- Date, names of the parties (their assigns and successors in business) to the contract, and the book's title.
- Author's grant. The author usually grants the publisher the sole and exclusive licence and right to publish the book in all languages, for the full-term of copyright (author's life plus 50 years), throughout the world. By granting a licence, the author retains ownership of the copyright. Sometimes, however, authors (e.g. contributors to multi-authored books or to highly illustrated general books) assign their copyright, thereby passing ownership and all control to the publisher. Such authors may be paid one-off fees instead of royalties.
- Author's warranty. The author warrants that he or she controls the rights granted, that the work is original (not a plagiarism), does not contain defamatory, libellous or unlawful matter; and will indemnify the publisher for loss or damages etc.
- Competing works. The author agrees not to write a directly competing work for another publisher.
- Manuscript length, delivery date and form (e.g. two typescript copies, double spaced), and the responsibility for supplying illustrations and the index etc., and for obtaining and paying for third-party copyright material (often the author's responsibility unless otherwise agreed). The publisher reserves the right not to publish if the delivered manuscript is overdue or not fit for publication.
- Corrections. The author is constrained from making extensive corrections to proofs (other than those attributable to publisher or printer) and is charged if author's corrections exceed a specified percentage (e.g. 10%) of the cost of typesetting. The author must return proofs within two to three weeks.
- Publication. The publisher entirely controls the publication (its production/design, publicity, price, methods and conditions of sale etc.). In practice authors may be consulted. The author is given say 6 gratis copies and may purchase more, not for re-sale, at a discount.
- Payments to authors: publisher's own-produced edition(s). Authors are normally (but not always) paid a royalty, expressed either as a percentage on an edition's published price ('list' or 'retail' price) on all copies sold; or as a percentage of the publisher's net receipts – its income (i.e. the sum of money received by the publisher after discounts have been deducted) on all copies sold. The author's earnings are thus proportional to price (or net receipts) and sales. Royalty rates

are quoted for the publisher's own-produced edition(s) (hardback or paperback, generally lower on paperback) on sales made in the traditional home market (the UK and Ireland) and in export markets (export rates are lower to take account of the higher discounts involved).

A scale of royalties rising by steps of 2–2$\frac{1}{2}$% when certain quantities have been sold may be included (especially on home market sales). Royalty rates on published price range from say 5 to 15% (many authors never surpass the lower base rates). If an author has attained a higher rate and a new edition is produced, the royalty reverts to the base rate. When the book is remaindered, no royalties may be paid. Other provisos where lower royalties apply are stated.

- Payments to authors from rights sales. The contract lists further rights granted to the publisher (unless otherwise agreed) which it could license to other firms, and the percentages (e.g. 50–90%) payable to the author on the publisher's net receipts from such sales. If the publisher is granted, for example, US, book club and translation rights, the firms to which these rights could be licensed may print their own editions and pay royalties to the publisher to be shared with the author. However the publisher may print bulk quantities for them to appear under the licensees' imprints. The publisher sells such copies at a high discount and the author's royalty may be inclusive of the sum received (e.g. 10%). There are many other rights such as serial and extract rights; dramatization rights on stage, film, television and radio; broadcast reading rights; quotation and anthology rights; digest condensation; mechanical reproduction rights (e.g. on audiocassette); electronic media publishing rights etc. All or some of these rights may be termed 'subsidiary rights'.
- Accounting. The publisher's accounting period to the author is usually 6 months for general books, or annual for educational and academic books, with settlement 3–4 months after.
- Revisions. The author agrees to revise the book when requested or to permit others to do so at the author's expense.
- Termination. The rights revert to the author (e.g. if on request the publisher fails to keep the work in print).
- Arbitration in dispute.
- Option. The author may give the publisher the right of first refusal on his/her next book.
- Author's moral rights.
- Special provisions, such as an advance on author's royalties.
- Signatures of the parties.

THE DIVISION OF ENGLISH LANGUAGE RIGHTS

Traditionally, the UK and US publishers (especially consumer) have been in separate ownership and have divided the world English book market between them. For books published on both sides of the Atlantic, the UK and US publishers seek exclusive market areas (closed markets) from which the other's competing editions are excluded. The US publisher's exclusive territory was essentially the USA; the UK publisher's the Commonwealth, Ireland and South Africa and a few others, the remaining areas being non-exclusive to either (the open market, such as mainland Europe) where UK and US editions of the same book are in direct competition. Canadian rights were exclusively retained by UK publishers on their own originated books, and by US publishers on theirs. For some books this broad division still persists and can affect the way agents and packagers grant rights to publishers, and the way publishers trade books between themselves. For example, a UK publisher holding world rights could either sell its own edition to the USA through its related US firm (or by a distribution arrangement); or license the rights to a separate US publisher, in which case the US publisher's exclusive, non-exclusive, and excluded territories would be negotiated. Conversely a UK publisher may buy a US originated book from a US publisher or author represented by an agent, and its rights and territories, too, would be so defined.

This traditional territorial split of exclusive, non-exclusive (open market) and excluded territories is threatened from many quarters. The advent of the EC single market principle of free movement of goods is in conflict with the traditional UK/US publishers' contracts whereby the UK is an exclusive territory and mainland Europe is open. The greatest fear of UK publishers is that the UK market itself would potentially become flooded with cheaper US editions imported from mainland Europe, negating the UK publishers' exclusive contractual and market rights. Such 'parallel' importation is unlikely to occur from direct breaches of contracts by US publishers, but at the hands of third-party traders based in the USA or Europe who are not themselves parties to the UK/US publishers' agreements. US publishers have the great advantage of a very much larger and richer unified home market. They thus benefit from long print runs, with lower unit (i.e. cost per copy) production costs allowing generally lower book prices.

Apart from price differentials between competing editions (which are influenced by £/$ exchange rates with local European currencies), the time of the release of different editions of the same title is another factor. US and UK consumer book publishers deploy the strategy of maximizing earnings through the sequential publication of a particular book in different formats and prices. For example, first publication would be in a higher priced hardback, followed by a paperback, and possibly by accident or design, by a remainder or bargain book edition. In export markets, especially the growing mainland European market, UK and US publishers attempt to pre-empt the other's competing edition in paperback while maintaining their home markets for a period exclusively in hardback. Hence UK export editions of mass market paperbacks are available earlier on mainland Europe than in the UK, and can be bought on the air-side of UK airports. Mainland European paperback importers may hedge their bets by simultaneously ordering their stock from both US and UK publishers to ensure they receive stock from whichever is the earliest. Importers also compare the prices of competing editions, and scout around for bargain priced editions.

Therefore the UK publishers argue with the American publishers that the European Union and additional countries joining it should be treated as a single market and that it should be the exclusive territory of UK publishers, in the same way as the US unified market is treated. The ultimate aim of the world's international publishers is to be strong enough in all main countries through direct ownership enabling them to acquire and control exclusive world rights in authors' copyrights thereby overcoming legislative difficulties anywhere in the world and ameliorating 'buying around' practices of third-party traders.

AUTHORS' AGENTS

Literary agents, now called authors' agents (reflecting the broad range of authors they represent), are mostly located in the London region giving them close proximity to their main customers – fiction and non-fiction editors, mainly in adult but also in children's book publishers. Their business is selling rights to a variety of media (not just book publishers) at home and abroad on behalf of their client authors. Agents receive a commission on authors' earnings, at the bare minimum 10% but rising to 15–20%, especially on deals made abroad. Owing to increased administrative and sales costs, minimum commissions have crept upwards.

Agents represent many of the established professional writers (i.e. those who derive much of their income from writing). While some agents are prepared to review unsolicited manuscripts from aspiring novelists for which they may charge a reading fee, others discourage this practice and take on new clients only on personal recommendations from credited sources, such as publishers. Rarely is it worth while for an agent to represent academics unless their work appeals to a wide readership.

An agent manages a writer's career primarily from a commercial viewpoint, for example by placing the author's work with the right publisher or fuelling competition between publishers; negotiating contracts to secure the best terms; checking or querying publishers' advance payments against royalties, royalty statements and chasing debts.

The example of the contract summarized on page 49 shows the author granting various world rights to the publisher. Because most authors are unable to market the rights on their work worldwide they mainly allow publishers to do so on their behalf. But an agent representing an author may limit the rights granted to a publisher, and their territorial extent, and sell the rights retained on behalf of the author to other firms at home and abroad. For instance, the UK publisher's licence may apply to the English language only, and the territory (the countries) in which it has the exclusive right to publish (e.g. the Commonwealth and Europe) are listed, as well as those from which it could be excluded (e.g. the USA, including/excluding Canada). An agent could then license the book to a US publisher directly. A UK publisher, within its exclusive territory, could for instance be granted the following rights: the right to publish a hardback and a paperback; and to license to others book club, reprints, second and subsequent serial (i.e. extracts appearing after book publication in newspapers etc.), quotation and anthology, mechanical and reproduction, broadcast reading rights etc. (the income from which is shared with the author). An agent retains, for instance, foreign language translation, first serial (extracts appearing before book publication giving a newspaper scoop), stage/radio/television/film dramatization rights etc. However, there is no clear-cut division of rights or territories covered – each book differs. A publisher which has the idea for the book and contributes much editorial and design effort has a strong case for acquiring wide territorial rights and the sharing of other rights. Adult and children's publishers and packagers producing highly illustrated books for the international market need world rights in all languages. Book packagers and some highly illustrated book publishers often acquire the copyright outright from authors enabling subsequent re-packaging and recycling of authors' material without further payment or author contact.

UK agents retaining rights may sell them directly to, for example, US publishers or film companies or continental publishers, or use overseas agents with whom they have arrangements. Conversely, UK agents may represent well known American authors on behalf of US authors' agents, and sometimes US publishers via their rights sales managers. The selling of rights from a publisher's viewpoint is described in Chapter 4; an agent's work is similar except that an agent solely represents the author.

The additional dimension of agents' work falls under an editorial heading. For instance, agents send out synopses and manuscripts for external review, comment on manuscripts and advise authors on what they might write and the media they might write for, and develop ideas with them; or be asked by publishers to supply authors; or initiate projects themselves for sale to publishers.

Agents can provide a degree of continuity in the face of changing publishers and editors. However, some authors decide to change agents. The former agent continues to receive commission on existing contracts which can conceivably endure for decades after the author's death. The long established agencies manage the literary estates of classic authors whose work remains in copyright.

Many agents operate from home as single person companies. The few large agencies consist of a range of agents each of whom specializes in broad areas of books or the selling of particular rights, though each agent usually looks after a particular primary group of authors. Some of their assistants show sufficient aptitude to develop their own list of authors, and new agents arise from one-time rights sales staff and editorial staff of publishers.

BOOK PACKAGERS

Such firms, usually small and founded by an editor or designer or sales person, tend to produce mainly highly illustrated and saleable, expensive to produce, informational colour hardbacks which are published and marketed under the imprints of other firms (chiefly adult and children's general publishers, and book clubs). They may supply own-brand books for bookselling chains and supermarkets; bargain books for promotional publishers; and books and colour brochures for other businesses. A few packagers produce illustrated school textbooks, or mixed or multimedia English language teaching courses, or dictionaries, encyclopaedias or atlases etc. Packagers are discreetly named on a book's copyright page.

They provide a customer with creative editorial, design and production expertise which would be too difficult or expensive to sustain in-house. Sometimes packagers are commissioned to produce the books. But more frequently packagers initiate projects and try to pre-sell bulk quantities of books to publishers usually on an international co-edition basis, often restricting the exclusive territorial rights granted to a UK publisher and other rights. For example, before the book is written and created, the packager shows publishers the book's synopsis, specimen material, mock-ups of printed pages, dummy and cover. Their aim is to secure orders for sufficient quantities and up-front payments from a UK publisher (sometimes with book club support), and usually from a US publisher to cover the direct development costs spread over the first printing of several imprint editions. Further English language reprints and foreign language co-editions printed for publishers should bring in the profit.

Packagers may become frustrated by the lack of sales effort given to their books, which they have created and sold to UK publishers, and the tight margins they are put under. Thus some packagers take the risk of becoming publishers in their own right in the UK market while continuing to sell co-editions abroad. Packagers, like some small publishers, may overstretch themselves and go bust. The selling of international co-edition books by packagers and publishers can be a volatile market depending as it does on the vagaries of American, Australian and European publishers, and of fluctuating exchange rates.

THE UK BOOK TRADE

The sales success of consumer books, especially, depends on retail exposure. *The Impulse Buying of Books* (1982) survey found that about half the books sold over the counter were on-the-spot impulse buys, and in the confectioner/tobacconist/newsagent (CTN) outlets, about three-quarters were impulse buys. Of possible factors prompting impulse purchase, 30% bought on the name of the author (higher with fiction buyers), 30% liked the look of the book, and only 13% related to the impact of publishers' marketing and recommendations by the bookshop. Over 40% of impulse buys were made without any prior knowledge of the book or author.

About 90% of consumer books are sold through shops; thus publishers' main customers are the retailers, predominantly the bookselling chains, say, well over 40%; independent bookshops, 15–25% (mainly supplied by trade wholesalers fed by publishers); other retail and distribution channels, say, 20% plus; and the library suppliers. Publishers direct most of their marketing and sales effort at the booksellers, especially the major chains which devote much or most of their floorspace to books; others which are significant intermediaries (wholesalers and library suppliers); and, if engaged especially in the publishing of highly illustrated non-fiction and of children's books, additionally at other sales distribution channels.

The selling of consumer books via a variety of customers is very complex and is becoming more diverse. Books appear in many different kinds of non-book retailers (such as supermarkets etc.) and, to the consternation of stockholding booksellers, are sold in more visible discount price forms, such as through book clubs increasingly opening high street outlets (potentially through US-style out-of-town 'club' warehouses), and through bargain book chains and direct sales operations to consumers in the home, office and school.

Bookshops

The largest bookselling (multi-product/stationery) chain buys books centrally from a publisher's sales manager, and relates each title and quantity to a scale determined by the size and character of its branches. The books are distributed from a central warehouse. Publishers' sales representatives (reps) are denied access to the branches.

The major stockholding bookselling chains dedicated to books generally have central marketing departments (organizing consumer advertising, in-store book and author promotions etc.), and employ knowledgeable and motivated, graduate book buyers in their branches who are seen by publishers' reps. Key features of these large dedicated book stores are the breadth, depth and mix of titles stocked, and the importance of backlist sales (say, well over 60%) versus frontlist (i.e. new book) sales. For instance, their core stock backlist inventory can extend to upwards of 70 000 titles. The burrowing nature of book addicts enables such booksellers to utilize fully all floors, nooks and crannies, unlike most other retailers.

The independent chains and the larger independent booksellers and some smaller ones are visited by publishers' reps. But many small shops are not visited by reps and have thus lost contact with many publishers. They are supplied mainly by the trade wholesalers stocking around 50 000 titles and offering fast and efficient distribution. The advantages to the bookseller include dealing electronically with a few wholesaler suppliers rather than with dozens of publishers with their invoicing, and variable distribution systems, and avoiding minimum order quantities or minimum values imposed by some publishers. The trade wholesalers provide their bookshop customers with 'buy notes' on forthcoming titles, may supply non-book retail outlets and are entering the library supply market. Some trade wholesalers are expanding into supplying mainland European bookshops, offering prices more competitive than those of local wholesalers.

Other significant book outlets with which publishers have traditionally dealt directly include the respected book departments in major department stores; and airport terminal shops, especially Heathrow and Gatwick, which sell enormous quantities of paperback fiction, travel and business books. Flight delays of half-an-hour are a boon for book sales.

Technological advances in bookshops have affected publishers. Ordering by electronic means has helped speed up stock replenishment. The installation of Electronic Point of Sale (EPoS) systems reading the bar codes on covers enables booksellers to monitor the rate of sale of titles and to control their inventory and re-orders more exactly. In consequence, booksellers place smaller orders more frequently, and expect faster deliveries from publishers.

For the publishers of adult consumer books (but not of children's books), for the publishers of tertiary textbooks (but not of educational textbooks) and of many professional interest titles, the dedicated bookshops are the most important sales outlets. Good booksellers reach out to the local community, provide a platform for author and book promotions, may send out catalogues listing their new and stock titles to customers, foster links with associations and teaching institutions, are pro-active in their buying to suit their local customer profile, are knowledgeable about books and will order books for customers from among the 600 000 backlist titles in print.

Bookshops, however, are a narrow channel to reach the general public, of whom perhaps upwards of 70% never venture into them. There are around 1500 bookshops of reasonable size, of which some half significantly influence the pattern of book buying, and a smaller number, say 500, are the main retailers of non-fiction. There is a view that regular book buyers when presented with a wide range of interesting books in an attractive bookshop facilitating browsing will buy more books, while people not used to book buying would be baffled by choice and intimidated by the setting. But if such people are presented with a very narrow choice, in a non-bookshop setting, they would be more likely to purchase a book on impulse. (Focusing the public's attention on a selected and small number of recommended titles has long been the fundamental strategy of book clubs.)

Non-book outlets

It is estimated that books are sold in upwards of 47 000 other outlets, in which books form only a minor part of the product range, the stocking decisions are taken externally to the outlet itself, the staff have little or no knowledge of the books themselves, and at the check-out no customer orders are taken.

The major customers of the mass-market paperback fiction publishers have been for many years the large wholesale merchandisers servicing the vast number of the CTN outlets. These wholesalers buy centrally from the publisher and scale out the books in relation to the number of 'pockets' in the outlets, some of which may be bookshops. Their merchandisers, carrying the stock in vans, regularly replenish the outlets with new books and remove slow-selling titles for destruction. Their contract business has extended over time into other kinds of outlets such as convenience general stores, petrol stations and ferry port outlets, motorway service stations (where gifts and male-orientated books tend to be placed at high traffic points close to the lavatories), department and variety stores; and especially to supermarkets needing, for instance, a more female-orientated mix, supplementing their own-brand titles produced for them by highly illustrated book publishers, children's publishers and packagers. The supermarkets are attracted to the higher discounts and no risk, sale or return, features of the book business. Some publishers sell direct to supermarkets. The range of books merchandised has also extended including reference, best-selling children's titles and highly illustrated books.

There are 'more specialist' kinds of wholesale merchandisers pushing out the frontiers of related book availability into, for example, garden, DIY, and leisure centres, and to specialist shops such as chemists, alternative medicine, haberdashery, wine, food, gift and toy shops, computer stores etc. A few publishers, particularly in the highly illustrated sector, have developed their own merchandising arms.

Children's books

The children's book market has undergone radical change with under a third of sales through retail bookshops. Children's books sell well when displayed face out alongside other kinds of products such as in the multi-product/stationery chains (particularly the largest), or among groceries or toys especially where parents or relations have children in tow. The books are supplied through library/institutional suppliers, children's and school book clubs, school's leisure market suppliers, supermarkets (own-brand and non-exclusive titles), toyshops and retail learning centres, specialist wholesale merchandisers, direct selling operations and to a minor extent trade book wholesalers.

Although school library budgets are under great pressure, the school with its parents is an important outlet for children's books. The school provides a setting where children's books leap through the adult sales barrier and in which important word-of-mouth recommendations among children themselves take place. School book fairs have grown enormously and involve the supplier providing the school with upwards of 300 titles displayed face out, the school benefiting from a sales commission or free books. Moreover, school bookshops run by teachers and more linked to in-school reading acquisition, provide deeper access to publishers' backlists.

Bargain bookshops

The recession of the early 1990s witnessed considerable growth in bargain bookselling chains, selling remainders (UK and US titles) and bargain or 'promotional' books specially prepared for this market. They occupy high-street positions, sometimes on short-leases granted by stressed landlords. Conventional 'full price' booksellers also incorporated bargain book tables in their product mix, thereby helping to widen their customer profile among non-regular book buyers.

Publishers have a long history ridding themselves albeit quietly of their mistakes in overstocking, of printing too many copies. When a title's sales are insufficient to cover the cost of storage, it may be pulped or remaindered. Some publishers never remainder in the home market, or at all. A publisher having sold a book to a book club is restrained from remaindering. Remainders commonly stem from speculative or poor or disastrous publishing decisions on new books, or from the one reprint too many of good books. While a title may no longer sell in hardback or paperback at full price, it may sell well when released at a bargain price.

A publisher's sales manager sells the titles to a remainder dealer usually at a price well below the cost of manufacture. The dealer sells them on to bargain booksellers and to conventional booksellers, at say three times that price. The booksellers, who cannot return such books, sell them to the public at any price. A publisher may remainder only part of the stock (partial remaindering); for example if the publisher has a one-year stock plan and holds two years' stock, the balance is off-loaded to free warehouse space. A publisher may find the cost of reprinting too much and thus do a joint reprint with a dealer who shares the cost and the print run. On a 'put deal' a publisher, before publication, may find a dealer who agrees to take a quantity after a set period at a pre-determined price, provided the publisher is unable to sell them itself.

The promotional book publishers provide the bargain chains with a ready supply of newly created low-priced books.

Library suppliers

The public, academic and commercial libraries are supplied by booksellers and library suppliers; the latter with their own reps, offer a range of bibliographic services. The library suppliers export, especially academic and STM titles, sometimes under contract to national and governmental libraries, university research, specialist institution and to corporate libraries. They may also offer subscription services worldwide.

Some booksellers supply home and overseas customers by mail order, especially in specialist subject areas.

Publishers' discounts

Publishers sell their books to all these firms at different discounts off the published price, each publisher's discounts varying; and these firms constantly seek higher discounts – the more powerful the firm the greater the leverage. Consumer books have a greater discount range. For instance the small bookshops receive the lowest discounts (e.g. 32–37%); the bookselling chains seek 40% plus, and the largest with centralized buying and distribution receive the hardback wholesale rates of 45% to 50% plus; the paperback wholesalers seek 50–55%, up to 60% in mass-market paperback. The public library suppliers seek 40%, and, say, 50–55% on sheets which they bind in strengthened bindings. Broadly speaking, the academic/STM publishers offer textbook discounts of around 30–37% to retailers, and lower discounts down to 20% on high-level books supplied through bookshops. Some publishers discourage small orders by lowering the discount or imposing a surcharge. School textbooks are supplied directly to schools or via bookshops, specialist school contractors and local authority direct purchasing organizations on an average 17–20% discount. Schools receive a discount on the published prices of books supplied.

Book clubs

About 10% of the consumer book market is mail order mainly via book clubs and to a far less extent by booksellers' and publishers' mail-order. The general hardback book clubs, with around two million members, are the largest, while the membership of the more recently established paperback clubs numbers around several hundred thousand. There are other more specialist clubs such as children's book clubs, school book clubs and business book clubs. Generally speaking, book clubs recruit their members (who are required to buy a minimum quantity of titles at separate times) by large-scale consumer advertising offering deeply discounted 'premium offers', though they may recruit members from high street club centres and in people's homes. Their biggest problem is retaining members. Publishers supply the clubs with bulk quantities of books at very high discounts, and club discounted editions are distinguishable from trade (i.e. bookshop) editions. Sometimes book clubs print their own editions (see Chapter 4 for the selling of book club rights).

Direct selling operations

The recession of the early 1990s encouraged the expansion of direct selling, and on-site 'book club', operations selling usually discounted highly illustrated books via commission agents who take books into the office or factory for colleagues to pursue or who hold home parties etc.

THE NET BOOK AGREEMENT

The Net Book Agreement (NBA) or the resale price maintenance (r.p.m.) of books by another name, which had endured throughout the century, collapsed in September 1995. Under the agreement publishers had been free to designate a title a 'net book' or a 'non-net book'. When a title was designated a net book, the publisher set the book's net price, which in effect, and under the agreement, meant that retailers must maintain that price when they re-sold it to their customers. In other words, a retailer would not sell the book below the price set by the publisher. A retailer could charge more for the book (as sometimes happened on low margin educational or specialist titles) but overwhelmingly books were sold at the prices set by publishers and thus were not reduced in price or discounted by booksellers. When a publisher designated a title a non-net book the publisher still stated its published price (off which the retailer's discount was sprung) but the retailer was free to sell it at any price it wished, at a discount, at full price or whatever. Traditionally, the main designated non-net book category had been educational text-books supplied in class-sets to schools; and, in practice, remain-ders. The members of The Publishers Association (PA) who were signatories of the NBA ensured that retailers did not discount their net books and the PA enforced the NBA on their behalf.

The purpose of the NBA was to create a well-ordered book market in which a large number of dedicated booksellers could afford to stock a wide range of new and backlist titles, and to offer free customer services, sure in the knowledge that they could not be undercut by predatory retailers taking the cream off the narrow range of current bestsellers and fast-selling back-list stock titles.

By the mid-1990s, some leading consumer book publishers had abandoned net pricing and appeared to be gaining advantage as some major supermarket chains and booksellers deeply dis-counted their titles. Moreover the loss of consensus amongst publishers and booksellers to defend the NBA against uncertain and expensive legal proceedings before the UK courts and the European Commission meant that the PA could no longer enforce it. However, the arguments for and against the NBA before its demise continued in the aftermath.

Pro-NBA arguments maintained that it served the public interest because without it dedicated stockholding bookshops would be at risk, that they would be reduced in number and that the remaining booksellers would concentrate on a narrower range of titles. Book sales would fall as readers cast around for bargains, putting off immediate impulse purchases. Furthermore it contended that book prices would rise. A bookseller discount-ing some of the best-selling titles would not be able to recoup sufficient loss in margin from increased unit sales thus would have to recoup its margin elsewhere by increasing the prices of other books (including possibly textbooks) which might lead to a fall in demand, further lack of retail exposure, lower print runs and hence still higher prices recommended by publishers. Pressures on publishers' margins might increase still further as booksellers sought higher discounts. In turn, the consumer book publishers might well be expected to negotiate lower royalty rates with authors. Here, the cultural arguments came into play in relation to the plurality of books publicly available.

Without the protection under the NBA afforded to dedicated booksellers, independent booksellers might go out of business at a faster rate than was already occurring. The bookselling chains in conducting a price war to the death of the weakest and in competition with non-book retailers might change their nature. For instance, in order to cut their cost base, the dedicated book-selling chains might adopt centralized buying (in effect just like the old USSR where a handful of people determined what the public would read); rely on reactive EPoS data for re-orders; de-skill and downgrade their employees; and charge for customer services. Small publishers producing more specialist books might find access to the remaining chains difficult. Monopoly capital-ism in the form of greater concentration of ownership and control in publishing and bookselling, combined with the perceived increased difficulty of publishing books of minority and scholarly (not elitist) value, would thus impoverish the cultural, edu-cational and democratic diversity of the nation.

The anti-NBA arguments countered that r.p.m. was an anach-ronism in today's world where market forces should be left to take their free course (in other industries r.p.m. and associated cartels had long since been swept away, to the public benefit). Far from promoting books sales, it was suggested that the NBA inhibited active promotions on price, and a whole host of other normal marketing techniques such as vouchers, two books-for-the-price-of-one, on-pack and gift-with-purchase, etc. Why should dedicated booksellers, facing discounted books offered by book clubs, by direct selling operations and supermarkets' cheap own-brand titles, not be able to compete against them by offering their own discounts? In so doing dedicated booksellers would be able to broaden the book market themselves by attract-ing more non-regular book buyers into their stores.

Abolitionists argued that only a small fraction of titles pub-lished would be discounted, that increased competition on price would result in higher book sales, that the bookselling chains would survive and even if they did adopt centralized buying, the independent bookshops would be able to compete through specialization and customer care. The dedicated booksellers would be able to compete against book clubs and non-book retailers on a more equal footing. The former segmentation of the home market whereby most books had been sold at full price in most bookshops which positively aided separate discounted book channels would be removed. Publishers would be more able to extend their wares into non-book outlets, thereby facilitating impulse buys by people not used to book buying and reading, and encouraging such people subsequently to visit bookshops. Publishers would be able to compete more vigorously against other kinds of product, and against potentially growing numbers of cheap US book imports. No doubt the public would like to see really good books at bargain prices, not just recycled material. Book readers and institutional purchasers ultimately decide whether books are published. If they are not prepared to pay possibly higher prices for more esoteric and specialized books, then such books would not be published; if they are they would be.

Immediately following the demise of the NBA a price war broke out as retailers drastically cut prices of selected fiction and non-fiction hardback and paperback bestsellers; and some publishers offered trade discounts off their recommended retail prices of 60 per cent or more. The non-consumer book publishers were initially little affected. Meanwhile, the important publishers and booksellers in mainland Europe (most of which adopt their own forms of r.p.m.) generally re-affirmed their customs.

4

The process and the people

Under the editorial director are commissioning editors (sometimes termed sponsoring or senior editors), each responsible for finding, developing and matching marketable ideas with good authors, and for new editions (especially in reference and textbook publishing). Each editor, the main contact between author and publisher, builds a list of books that is part of, or composes, an imprint.

In consumer book publishing, editors may cover adult fiction and non-fiction, or either, or specialize in hardback or paperback lists, or in non-fiction areas, or children's books etc. In educational, academic and STM houses, an editor concentrates on several subjects spanning a variety of academic levels and markets. While editors work within a brief, the style and identity of each list are the outcome of the editor's attitudes and effort.

A publisher depends on these editors to provide a sufficient flow of publishable manuscripts to maintain its projected level of activity (say 15–30 new books annually per editor, sometimes far less or three times more). Moreover, editors are assessed on the overall profit-contribution of their books. Editors out of tune with senior management regarding the character of the books, or who fail to produce a profit, leave.

Some major exceptions apart (most notably in fiction) editors do not assess titles for publication on their thorough reading of complete manuscripts. Most books (including some fiction) are commissioned from authors on the basis of an outline, or specimen material. Furthermore most editors do not edit in detail the author's work – that is usually done by freelances or junior in-house staff. However, the senior editors may structurally edit by giving authors substantive criticisms and suggestions to help them produce their best work and to shape it for the intended market.

Editorial contacts and general market research

Good personal contacts are paramount. An editor's in-house contacts are the members of senior management who accept or veto projects; the people who produce the books (copy-editors, designers and production staff); and those who promote and sell them. But more significant are the editor's external contacts.

Prime sources of new books are the firm's previously published authors. They often have new ideas, or editors suggest ideas to them which are developed jointly.

In consumer book publishing, editors try to establish a mutual trust with literary agents (over lunch). Agents may send fiction manuscripts or non-fiction proposals to selected editors one at a time, or increasingly, to many editors simultaneously, or sometimes conduct auctions on highly saleable titles. Conversely an editor may contact an agent if she or he is after one of the agent's authors, or has an idea and wants an agent to find an author.

Fiction editors may also try to find new talent by spotting people who can write well, not necessarily fiction, or who are being published poorly or in an uncommercial medium.

The non-fiction editors who develop contacts in a variety of fields, constantly keep an ear to the ground, notice people's enthusiasms, review the media for topical subjects, try to predict trends or events which will be in the public's interest, monitor successful book categories and either avoid the competition, imitate it, or attempt to find unfilled niches by developing a new twist. They may write speculatively to people who have or may capture the public's imagination. In specialist fields, clubs and societies and their magazines can be sources of ideas and authors, and indicate level of interest. Editors interested in television and film tie-ins keep abreast of new productions and monitor audience ratings.

Editors forge links with other firms from whom they might buy or sell to, for example at the Frankfurt Book Fair. UK editors are in contact with US editors and rights sales managers, and UK reprint paperback editors are in contact with agents and hardback publishers' editors and rights managers on both sides of the Atlantic. Children's book editors have contact with teachers and librarians, and if producing illustrated colour books know US and foreign language publishers' editors and rights managers with whom they might trade.

The educational, academic, STM and professional book editors publish for more defined markets on which more statistical information is available (e.g. student enrolments, and numbers of researchers or professionals working in specific fields). However, these editors, apart from reading school syllabuses, college prospectuses and the relevant journals, are essentially engaged in direct market research and product development.

The academic and STM publishers often retain for each discipline exclusive advisers (senior academics or professionals with worldwide contacts) who direct new writers to their publishers. These publishers and educational publishers also enlist external expert general or series editors (also deployed by consumer book publishers) whose task is to help publishers' editors develop and edit the books. They usually receive a small royalty.

But the main thrust is understanding the current and future market on the ground. Educational editors see local education subject advisers, inspectors, examiners and lecturers in teacher training colleges; school heads and teachers using the materials in the classroom; and attend conferences. ELT editors, in addition to UK contacts, travel abroad and visit the Ministries and Institutes of Education, major Private Language Schools, offices of the British Council, local publishers and distributors etc. in order to fulfil the educational needs within specific cultures, and to assess market potential and credit-worthiness.

Academic, STM and professional book editors, may spend say several days a week visiting institutions and interview teaching staff in order to discover subject trends and market size, to find out their activities and views on books available, to flush out any ideas and contacts they have and to sell the firm's books. They may forge links with institutions, societies, industrial organizations etc. for which they could publish or distribute books or journals. When large US sales are anticipated, editors shape the material in conjunction with US publishers. All editors attend relevant conferences.

Unsolicited ideas and manuscripts

Hopeful authors bombard all publishers with unsolicited approaches. Consumer firms, which may reject over 99 per cent, employ part-time readers who sort through the 'slush' pile, write reports on possible ones and refer them to the editors. Most academic theses, too, sent direct to editors are unpublishable as they stand, but a few can be turned into monographs. It is very unlikely that an unsolicited textbook manuscript would be structured commercially, but occasionally unsolicited ideas can be developed.

The decision to publish

Many factors influence an editor's decision to pursue a new project, including:

- Suitability for list. A title has to fit the style and aims of the list for which it is known so that it is compatible with the firm's particular marketing systems. Furthermore, editors assessing new titles with other titles are concerned with the list's overall balance, direction and degree of innovation.
- Author assessment. The author's qualifications, motivation and time available to write the book, public standing, reliability to deliver on time, and responsiveness to suggestions.
- Market. The main audience for which the book is intended, who would buy it, the possible take-up at home and overseas. (The sales records on the author's previous books or those of similar books may be used as a guide.) Sometimes the rights sales potential is assessed (e.g. licensed book club, US rights), as well as special marketing opportunities on which the book could be promoted.
- Competition. The title's main selling points and advantages compared with the firm's own and competitors' books (e.g. especially textbooks and reference books).
- Content. The editor's judgement on the quality and appropriateness of the content is aided by others. Fiction editors may use junior editors, or external readers, to supply plot synopses or to offer first or second opinions. Non-fiction editors may ask specialist external readers to comment on specialist titles. Other publishers rely heavily on experts (e.g.

teachers, academics, professionals) sometimes worldwide to comment on material initially, during or after the book has been written. (All these external readers are paid small fees and remain mostly anonymous to the author.)

- Book's physical appearance and price. The editor envisages a proposed title's desirable physical form (e.g. its word length, illustration content, size, binding style and production quality), the likely cost and the price range within which it could be sold.

Some ideas are rejected, especially on unfavourable reports; some authors are asked to re-submit in the light of editors' suggestions; others are pursued. An editor cannot offer a contract without the agreement of the senior management. Editors sound out and lobby senior colleagues, such as the home and export sales managers, over possible prices and sales forecasts and the production manager over the production costs. The editor prepares a publishing proposal form (circulated) which covers the scope of the book, its form, its market and competition, readers' reports, publication date, reasons for publication etc. Additionally, a financial statement sets the expected sales revenue against the costs of producing the book and those of author's royalties to give the hoped-for profit margin – provided the book sells out. Different combinations of prices and sales forecasts, and of print-run production costs and of royalties, may be tried. Many publishers hold formal meetings at which the main departmental directors hear editors' proposals – most get through, but some are referred back or rejected.

The editor, given the go-ahead, negotiates the contract with the author or agent (agents present their own contracts weighted in the author's favour), agrees or invents the book's title (important for sales success), and on commissioned books ensures that the author appreciates what is expected (e.g. content, length, deadline). There may be an optimum publication date which would maximize sales (e.g. a consumer book that is topical or published for the Christmas market; or textbooks of which bound copies are needed for inspection by teachers ideally around the new year to secure adoptions in the northern hemisphere and April-June for the southern). Some authors submit chapters for comment; others deliver the complete manuscript on time or later (or never). The manuscript is checked for length, completeness and quality (may be again externally reviewed), may be returned or accepted and is then handed down the line. The book is costed again.

Editors brief and liaise with junior editors, designers, production, promotion and sales staff and may write the blurb (the first twenty words of which must grip the reader). Although editors have no managerial control over other departments, they endeavour to ensure their books receive due attention. The editors present their books to the publisher's sales force at the regular sales conferences.

Some editors, especially those involved with complex and highly illustrated books, or major textbook projects, get very involved in the production stages.

At the page-proof stage, the book's published price is fixed, as well as the number of copies to be printed and bound. The number printed may be less or more than the number envisaged at the outset.

The editors' involvement with re-pricing, reprinting, pulping or remaindering decisions varies from firm to firm. In some, the sales director is the dominant force.

Skills

No editor can simply sit back and expect marketable ideas and authors to flow in. Building contacts and opportunities takes initiative and quick-footed detective work to identify the sources of books, authors and ideas. Editors need to be creative in that they encourage and develop received ideas or initiate ideas themselves and match them to authors. Inevitably these lead up false trails, so editors have to be agile enough to hunt the front-runners.

Profitable publishing depends on a perception of trends in markets and timing (good editors pre-empt competitors – in textbook publishing the lead time can easily be three years); constant vigilance, inquisitiveness and receptivity to new ideas; and responsiveness to changing needs. In specialist fields it involves asking experts the right questions, and being aware of their personal prejudices, professional jealousies and ideological positions. The skill lies in choosing the right advisers/readers – and assessing the assessors.

The consumer book editors, who face great difficulty in ascertaining market needs, base their judgements on a combination of experience of what sells, having a finger on the pulse, and intuition. Backing one's own hunches takes considerable audacity and confidence.

Fundamental to book and author selection is the editor's ability to assess the quality of the proposal and of the author's writing and purpose. This critical faculty (underpinned by skills in speed reading and sampling sections of writing) develops from experience and intuitive discernment. Editors should be able to contribute to structural improvements, and in specialist areas appear to the author not merely as a cipher for expert readers' comments.

The authors, who supply the raw material on which the success of the enterprise is founded, are engaged in long spells of isolation when writing with little else to draw on but experience, knowledge and imagination. In their books rest their dreams and hopes. In their eyes the editor is exclusive to them; to the editor an author is one of many. Authors expect editors to represent their interests in-house, to get things done and judge editors on their in-house clout. Conversely editors must represent the best interests of the publisher to authors – at times a fine juggling act. Most authors are extremely sensitive about their work and the way it is published. Good editors persuade authors to write, foster author loyalty to the house, and nudge and encourage them in certain directions. Major skills lie in deciding when an author will appreciate intervention and its form, and in conveying constructive opinions honestly without damaging author self-confidence. Authors need encouragement, reassurance and praise – that, and the editor's diplomacy, are vital. Those authors who rely on their books for income (unlike teachers, academics etc.) centre their whole life around their writing. To some, an editor becomes inseparable from their private lives.

Editors need a knowledge of production methods (limitations and costs) and of contracts; the skill to negotiate with authors, agents and others; and the appreciation of the inter-relationships between costs and revenues, and the risk factors involved. They deploy politicing and manipulative skills (especially during the publishing proposal stage) and their infectious enthusiasm, selling and persuasive skills, used to promote the book's fortunes within the house, get communicated to the outside world.

DESK EDITING

Although a commissioning editor may edit manuscripts in detail, this work (desk editing) is usually done by junior and lower-paid in-house staff (variously known as desk, junior, assistant, house, or sub-editors) or, more often, by freelance copy-editors.

Those who undertake desk editing supervise the progress of books from manuscripts to bound copies, working closely with the production/design department, and giving information to marketing and sales people. They may copy-edit manuscripts and organize illustrations themselves; they may (or may not) edit manuscripts for overall clarity and pass them to freelance copy-editors for the detailed work. They subsequently send proofs to authors and to freelance proofreaders, collate corrections and generally oversee the book's production from an editorial standpoint. Some academic/STM book and journal publishers employ 'production editors' who are also responsible for the design and production stages.

Only in firms where job demarcations are drawn not too tightly, and where desk editors work specifically for sympathetic commissioning editors, is there the likelihood of commissioning experience, usually without responsibility. Below the desk editor level there may be editorial assistants or editorial secretaries: their work ranges from pure secretarial and administrative support to editorial work under supervision, such as proofreading, collating corrections, finding pictures for the text, applying for the clearance of third party copyright material, and handling reprints. In consumer book publishing, junior editorial staff may write reports on new book proposals.

Some publishers have a managing editor or supervisor who allocates, financially controls and supervises freelances' work, and there are production firms that offer that service to publishers. In some publishers the production department organizes the freelance editing and proofreading. Very few publishers retain a pool of copy-editors into which the manuscripts are fed.

Some educational, academic and STM publishers have introduced development editors who directly support the commissioning editors on major textbook projects. Such an editor carries out survey research in association with the marketing/sales departments in order to ascertain market needs, organizes the external reviewing of drafts and helps shape the project with the authorial team from conception to completion.

Manuscript editing

The aim of the copy-editor (who may be the only person other than the author who reads the book pre-publication) is to ensure that the text and illustrations are clear, correct and consistent for both the printer and the ultimate readers. The copy-editor is also usually expected to look out for libellous passages.

The copy-editor, who is briefed on the nature and market of the book, first needs to check that all the manuscript items handed over are indeed present and that they have been clearly labelled and numbered by the author (e.g. the typescript or hard-copy – sometimes with disks – and illustrations). The author is asked for any outstanding items, otherwise the book will be held up.

The work of copy-editing falls into three related processes.

- At the lowest order of detail, the task is to ensure that the author's text is consistent in such matters as spelling, hyphenation, capitalization, agreement of verbs and subjects, beginning and ending of quotation marks and parentheses, and many other points sometimes included in the firm's house style. The accuracy and relationship of parts of the text to others, such as in-text cross-references to illustrations, captions, chapters and notes, the matching of headings on the contents page to those in the text and of citations to the reference list etc. and the arrangement and preparation of pages with which authors may be unsure (e.g. the preliminary pages) are also this editor's concern. Each new book presents its own problems in the detailed handling of stylistic points, and decisions have to be made in regard to alternative ways of applying the rules, if at all.

- While some publishers restrict copy-editing to this level, others expect editors to a varying extent to engage in the second parallel editorial process, which may be termed substantive editing. This calls for clear perception of the author's intent and sometimes restraint from the copy-editor; but, where appropriate, attention is paid to discordant notes, such as obscure, incoherent, misleading or ambiguous sentences, or non sequiturs in factual passages; unintentional use of mixed metaphors or of repetition; unusual punctuation in sentence construction; paragraphing; over or under use of headings etc. Furthermore, authors' errors of fact, and inconsistencies, omissions, contradictions and illogicality in their argument or plot may be found. Substantive editing may thus entail the re-writing of sentences, reorganization, or suggesting other ways to present material.

Editors look out for abbreviations and terms unfamiliar to readers. The avoidance of parochialisms or culturally specific UK examples is especially important in books aimed for overseas. The avoidance of sexist, racist, ageist and classist language or values and of corresponding stereotypes are issues which confront editors, designers and illustrators, particularly those in educational and children's publishing. These staff also try to ensure that the level of language and of text and illustrations is appropriate for the intended age group.

- The third parallel editorial process carried out, whether the second substantive form is done or not, concerns indicating to the designer and/or typesetter, parts of the text that need special typographic treatment. Items so marked or coded include the italicizing of words in sentences, the indication of unusual sorts (e.g. letters with accents), the labelling of the heading hierarchy (e.g. chapter headings, section and sub-section headings) and the areas of text to be indented, displayed or typeset in sizes or faces different from the main text (e.g. long quotations, lists, notes, captions, tables etc.). In the absence of a designer, the editor may do the typographic mark-up as well.

Work methods

A common method involves the editor quickly looking through the manuscript to gain a measure of the author and the book. Ideally, decisions regarding the handling of stylistic points (e.g. spelling, hyphenation, capitalization, terminology) are taken at the outset. A style sheet is developed to aid consistency and memory – an editor deals with many titles at any one time – and helps proofreading, which may be done by someone else such as a freelance who may be other than the freelance copy-editor.

To a varying extent, house style editing and substantive editing conflict, in that concentration on one may lead to neglect of the other. Good editors go through manuscripts several times at different speeds focusing attention at various levels, moving back and forth during each examination.

During each examination editors make alterations on matters – especially those of house style – they believe to be right and defensible, but even so authors may disagree. Other changes and self-queries for later checking are marked on the manuscript or listed separately. Those that affect the design or production of the book, and which are in turn affected by the design and production methods, are addressed to the design or production department. Others, relating to content, may be addressed to the author.

If the author is contacted by telephone or in writing, editors need to be particularly tactful, explaining the kind of editing that has been done – perhaps by mentioning representative samples – raising matters needing assistance, reaching agreement on matters of concern. The edited manuscript may be returned to the author for checking. Alternatively, a meeting is held. The editor, for instance, by adopting the reader's viewpoint, and suggesting solutions, may persuade the author to make necessary changes.

Illustrations

The author may also need to resolve queries on illustrations. If the author cannot supply illustrations editors sometimes have to undertake picture research or brief a researcher. If the publisher is responsible for obtaining copyright permission, the editor or researcher writes to copyright holders. Each illustration or table is labelled and compared against the accompanying text and caption. Caption and source copy are prepared.

Drawn illustrations are prepared from copies of those previously published if suitably amended, or from author's original line work, roughs or ideas. They are edited for sense and consistency before being passed to the designer or illustrator who is briefed. Correction cycles follow. The desired position of the illustrations is indicated in the text.

Prelims

Preliminary material ('prelims') is drafted. It usually includes pages giving the book title and author, the name of the publishing house, copyright notice, International Standard Book Number (ISBN) – a unique number identifying the book – and may include a contents page, list of illustrations, acknowledgement of copyright material used, foreword etc. The Cataloguing in Publication (CIP) data (supplied by the British Library), sometimes included in prelims, is inserted later.

Cover copy —— /ad.

Printed covers or jackets are needed well in advance of the printed book for promotion and sales purposes. Thus the cover copy (e.g. title, author, blurb and ISBN) is passed to the designer preferably at this stage and the proofs checked later.

Conventional book production proof stages

Most unillustrated books (or those with only a few illustrations which are easily placed) go straight to page proofs. The typesetter re-keys the text, arranges the page breaks, inserts any illustrations, and returns proofs of pages numbered as they will finally appear. Proofs are normally read by the author and publisher (in-house or by freelances), and checked against the original copy. The corrections and improvements are collated by the editor and inserted by means of standard symbols on one master set (the marked set). Correction marks are colour-coded (e.g. red for typesetter's errors, blue for author's and publisher's) so that costs can be apportioned. (Publishers may charge authors for excessive corrections.) The marked set returns to the typesetter for correction, and unless second proofs of problem pages are requested, the book is passed for press. *depends on imgs*

Books with many illustrations integrated with the text follow a different path. The typesetter returns galley proofs which are merely unpaged text proofs. While these are being read, the artwork is finalized and photographs collected. The designer checks the text typography and taking account of deletions or additions to the text proof and the planned size of illustrations lays out the pages of the book by means of a paste-up. On to the grid of facing pages, the designer pastes photocopies of the amended galleys and indicates the position of the sized illustrations (e.g. by empty rectangles or photocopies) and other elements. The editor checks the paste-up, if necessary amending the text to fit the layout, and inserts the picture credit copy and page numbers on the contents page etc.

The typesetter follows the marked galley proof for the textual changes, and uses the paste-up as a guide to the page make-up. The typesetter, or another firm, reproduces the illustrations to the specified size. (Sometimes high quality illustration proofs, especially of colour, are requested for checking against the originals.)

The page proofs return and are checked by the author and publisher against the first proofs and paste-up. Further proofs may follow.

New technology and desktop publishing

In conventional book production, the edited and marked-up manuscript is sent to a typesetting firm or printer where it is re-keyed on a computer, editorial changes inserted and the typo-graphic design enacted. Typeset proofs return which contain new errors. But increasingly, authors hand publishers disks accompanied by hard-copy. The editorial changes, and codes that will determine the typography, may be inserted on disk, by the editor; by an in-house keyboarder; by a computer bureau or the typesetter.

Some authors believe book publishers have been slow in adopting new technology. However, publishers receive disks from authors using a variety of hardware and software, software which is sometimes outdated and which often has to be con-verted and reformatted. Meanwhile publishers' suppliers, the typesetters at home and abroad, have in real terms drastically reduced the costs of re-keyed typesetting. Moreover, typesetters offer to take authors' disks along with the publisher's edited hard-copy, and carry out the disk conversion, coding, correction, and pagination processes, again at very low prices. Publishers can thus avoid investing in fast-dating hardware and software, and in-house staff training, and can continue to use low-cost freelances armed with pens. On any revised edition, the pub-lisher can ask the typesetter to update the text files. If that typesetter has gone out of business, another typesetter will type-set and insert changed paragraphs, or completely reset the book. Under these arrangements, the publisher's books are held in their final and correct digital form by a variety of external typesetters using various systems which are quite often incompatible. In wanting to hold and control its existing books in digital form, the publisher is faced with expensive options. A printed book may be passed through an optical character recognition machine which introduces errors; or the typesetter may be asked to return the text files which are reverse-engineered into the publisher's chosen system; or the book may be reset.

The impetus to adopt in-house electronic handling of manuscripts occurred first among publishers producing reference 'database' titles (especially dictionaries, allowing spin-off versions) or titles needing frequent updating; some journal publishers looking towards electronic transmission; and secondly among some book publishers or packagers producing highly illustrated information books. The latter especially are attracted to desktop publishing (DTP) systems deploying what-you-see-is-what-you-get (WYSIWYG) representation on screen and on paper. It allows designers to develop trial book designs and layouts at speed, and allows editors and designers to develop complex text and illustration pages before committing money to final typesetting.

In the drive towards adopting new technology, a publisher aims to quicken the production schedule and hence time taken to reach the market, to reduce production costs, to be able to address new publishing opportunities and itself to have the capability of re-using its intellectual properties.

In an ideal world, the author uses the same wordprocessing software as the publisher; that software is style-based (i.e. electronic codes are applied consistently to the various structural elements, e.g. to the hierarchies of headings and to lists, to kinds of paragraphs etc.); and the author is provided with a basic style sheet of electronic codes to follow. In the event of the author using different software, the publisher has to convert the author's disks to its own wordprocessing system. The conversion usually loses the author's formatting and introduces errors.

The publisher's copy-editor can mark-up the hard-copy of the manuscript in the traditional way for others to correct electronically; or edit on the hard-copy, or on screen or in combination, imposing the style codes against the textual elements, and making changes electronically. Software facilities such as spell checkers, and search and replace features aid editorial accuracy and consistency. The electronic design file usually generated in the production or design department is applied to the codes and enacts the typography – the typefaces, sizes, line lengths and spacing.

Technical line drawings and graphs etc. may be prepared electronically in different software programs and are merged with the text files. The book may be paginated in the wordprocessing program or with specialist software, and proofs are produced on laser printers for authors to check. The division of labour between editors, designers and production staff is inter-related but blurred.

The above process of **style coding** books enables the publisher to control and hold its books in electronic form and is especially appropriate for those titles, for instance textbooks, which are likely to be re-usable, i.e. there is a good expectation of a reasonable life through subsequent editions or versions. Style coding is also deployed by some of the main wordprocessing and DTP software suppliers. Moreover, such wordprocessing and DTP systems use a common page description language called Postscript, which tells the output device (such as an office laser printer or higher resolution typesetter) what to print and how to print it. Such output devices translate the page description into an arrangement of dots that represents the letters and images on the page, and the pulses of the laser beam in the output device match this 'map' dot for dot. The output is then used for the mass-production of printed pages.

While style coding is relatively straightforward and is a natural extension of editorial practices (e.g. the coding of headings), it is usually specific to particular software. Moving the styled document to another software program involves a translation and that may cause errors. Furthermore, style coding focuses on and has its routes in the design and layout of printed documents.

For those publishers embarking on highly re-usable products (such as dictionaries, yearbooks, some legal and medical material, and journals), from which different spin-off versions of various size or content are envisaged, or which are likely to be exploited in other publishing mediums (such as CD, floppy disk, fax delivery or on-line), style coding is likely to be inadequate. Each publishing medium requires its own layout.

Some publishers are selectively applying Standard Generalized Markup Language (SGML) to such products. The key idea of

SGML is that it should provide an international and standardized way of coding structural information that is independent of any particular make of system, be it software, hardware or output device. In other words, SGML coded information is highly portable between different systems and publishing mediums. SGML focuses on coding/flagging the structural inter-relationships between the elements. A publisher designing a major dictionary, for example, would identify the elements within the entries needing coding/flagging to allow subsequent spin-offs to be produced easily and quickly with minimal re-coding; while a learned journal publisher would code intensively all the elements at the head of an article thereby facilitating abstracting, indexing, cataloguing and electronic means of document delivery. SGML coding is much more complex than style coding and demands a deeper analysis of a text's structural elements. It remains to be seen whether the boffins of SGML in the USA and Europe can make SGML sufficiently easy to use across the text communication industries. An international standard only becomes a true standard when widely used. So far as book publishers are concerned, its impact beyond books which are best described as databases is slight.

Index

Serious non-fiction books should have objective indexes that anticipate readers' needs and expectations. The authors are often responsible for index preparation and the cost, and either do it themselves or are supplied with a freelance indexer, found by the desk-editor sometimes from the Society of Indexers. If not, the index is done in-house or by a freelance who is briefed. Indexes are prepared from a page proof and have to be edited and typeset at great speed because the publication date is close.

Skills

Getting on with authors and senior editors and other in-house staff, and briefing them are crucial skills. Agreeing changes with authors and getting them to return proofs on time takes tact, self-confidence, persuasion, tenacity and negotiation face-to-face, in writing or on the telephone.

Editing manuscripts and proofreading demands a meticulous

eye for detail, a retentive memory, sustained concentration, endurance, patience, commonsense detective work and an ability to check one's own and others' work consistently.

Copy-editing and proofreading skills can to some extent be learnt from books, but added to that must be an editor's sound grasp of grammar and spelling, and preparedness to look things up. Editors should be able to place themselves in the reader's mind whatever subject knowledge they hold.

The enhancement of an author's work involves not only a knowledge of current stylistic conventions and language, but also judgement on the desirability and extent of their application, recognizing when it is necessary or unnecessary to make changes. Breaking the 'rules' for effect is not restricted to fiction. Appreciating the intangible quality of the author's voice can be important, especially in children's books.

Although an editor needs an enormous capacity to soak up detail, the ability to examine the text's overall sense is equally important. Visual awareness is also valuable, especially in highly illustrated adult and children's publishing and packaging, and low-level textbook publishing. Knowledge and understanding of production processes and ways of minimizing costs at all stages are essential, as is clear marking of the text: misleading instructions, sloppy work and/or poor handwriting cause errors and expense. Wordprocessing skills are increasingly required.

A publisher's office is hardly conducive to concentration. Editors dealing with many books (all at different stages of production) are pressed by the production office to meet deadlines, and are constantly interrupted by colleagues wanting instant information. Good editors are unflappable, they set priorities, manage time efficiently, switch quickly from one activity to another, and expect crises.

PICTURE RESEARCH

Picture research (the selection, procurement and collection of illustrations of all kinds) usually lies with the editorial department. The number of in-house picture researchers is however very small. They are concentrated in some of the highly illustrated, non-fiction, adult and children's book publishers and packagers (where they may create a picture library), and the large educational houses. Some commission photographers. A publisher or packager may, however, use expert freelance researchers, who may specialize in particular subjects. Otherwise, picture research for the text or cover or both may be just part of an assistant's or secretary's work in an editorial or jacket/cover department.

A general working specification for a book is drawn up in the editorial department (e.g. title, author, publication date, print run, book's market and its territorial extent, number of pictures required, ratio of colour to black and white, page size and picture budget). The editor and/or the designer may either brief the picture researcher at the idea stage, before the author has completed the manuscript, or later. The brief can range from being very specific (the author or editor supplying a complete picture list citing most sources), less specific (just listing the subjects), to very vague (requesting pictures to fit the manuscript). It is vital for the researcher to clarify the brief, especially the specificity of pictures.

The researcher may read the outline or manuscript in order to generate a list of ideas for approval by the editor and the author or amend the picture list supplied by the author to something more feasible. An estimate of cost is produced, based on the researcher's experience and the researcher advises whether the time and budget allocated are realistic; and potential sources are listed.

The researcher cannot progress quickly with selection without knowing where to look for an image, and without contacts to telephone or write to, or visit personally.

Sources, both home and abroad, include museums, libraries, archives, commercial picture agencies, photographers, public relations departments, professional and tourist organizations, charities, private individuals etc. Some major collections are held on CD. Sources come from consulting directories and picture source books, museum and library catalogues, guide books, brochures, magazines, acknowledgement lists in books, foraging around reference libraries etc. Researchers build up personal contacts with picture libraries and agencies, interview photographers, visit photographic exhibitions, and form contacts abroad. They compile their own records, indexes and address books. Their knowledge accumulates with each assignment.

The criteria for selecting sources include the nature of the material required (subject range, type of material – colour or black and white, quality) and the service offered (accessibility, speed and reliability, terms and conditions restricting borrowing or use of material, costs).

With the list of potential sources compiled, the next task is to request and collect the pictures by telephoning, writing letters and visiting. Replies are reviewed, and the incoming material is logged and labelled with sources' names. The researcher responsible for the good care of the material, selects suitable items and quickly returns the rejects to avoid paying holding fees and to reduce the risk of loss. Some sources, unable to supply, may suggest others; otherwise the researcher tries alternatives. The sources of pictures held for further consideration are approached, if necessary, with a request for an extended holding period.

The researcher does the initial selection and rejection of the pictures from a large assortment. Among the criteria for selection are the picture's **editorial content** (e.g. does the picture make the points or convey the impression or mood the author/editor intended?); **composition** (which should give the content clarity and impact); **reproducibility** (tonal range, colour range and definition), bearing in mind the quality of paper and reproduction method to be used; **costs** (reproduction and holding fees, print fees if buying prints, search and loss/damage fees etc.).

Once the researcher has sufficient suitable photographs, the cost is estimated again and a meeting (or several meetings) held with the editor and designer (and sometimes the author) to make the next selection. It might be that the researcher has to find more pictures very quickly before the final selection is made. Photographs must be ready by galley-proof stage to enable the designer to start the paste-up. The researcher organizes the pictures for handover to the designer, and supplies the picture credit copy and information for the captions (provided by the sources of the photographs) to the editor.

The next task is to write to the sources for copyright permission to reproduce pictures, and to negotiate the fees. The researcher passes the suppliers' invoices for payment and calculates the total picture costs. After checking the page proofs (some sources want copies), the book is printed, and the final responsibility is to return the pictures to the sources when they come back from the printer.

Skills

While a degree level of education is not essential, some picture researchers have a fine arts degree, helpful in that this develops an appreciation of composition. Knowledge of foreign languages eases contact with overseas sources; and typing is essential.

Picture researchers are only as good as their source address books and accurate visual memories. They must keep up-to-date and use imagination in research, not just in visualizing fresh uses for remembered pictures but almost instinctively knowing where to start looking for pictures on any subject, thinking methodically, finding cheap sources, and having a dogged persistence to get into new areas, getting behind closed doors. It is vital to forge good relations with sources – on the telephone, in writing and face-to-face. Researchers need the ability to interpret the message the book is trying to convey and, during selection, to make critical judgements on technical possibilities and costs as well as on aesthetic values. An understanding of the complexities of copyright and permission fees backs up their knowledge of sources; and allied to budget consciousness are the skills of negotiation especially with commercial picture agencies. Researchers must have a neat and tidy mind, and a good filing system, not least to avoid incurring holding fees and to reduce the danger of very expensive originals going astray. As one art director put it, 'It's a fascinating job – creative as well as administrative and business-like.'

DESIGN

Most in-house designers are employed by medium to large publishers issuing complex illustrated books (e.g. illustrated adult and children's non-fiction or textbooks), and by the more established book packagers. They may work in a design department or in a production department, reporting directly to the production manager. The design manager, responsible for the overall style of all the firm's books, is concerned with the deployment of in-house and external services, budgets, scheduling and administration. In-house designers may be graded, the senior designers co-ordinating the junior designers' work; there may be design assistants; and some in-house designers specialize in particular lists (e.g. children's or craft books) or a series. In publishers where jackets/covers have great sales power (mainly consumer book publishers, particularly mass-market paperbacks) jacket/cover designers or art directors are employed solely or mainly for their creation.

Small publishers may ask a good printer to help with the design; and in some large firms issuing relatively straightforward books (such as adult fiction or some high-level academic or professional books), editors or production controllers may design the books while commissioning freelance designers for covers. The use of freelances or agencies to design books and/or covers is widespread. They are commonly commissioned by editors or production staff, and by in-house designers.

Designing of promotional material may be the responsibility of in-house book designers, or solely of designers attached to the promotion department; or freelance designers or agencies are commissioned by that department. The execution of artwork is mainly done externally. Only a few large publishers (such as those issuing technical works, atlases and guidebooks) have in-house technical illustrators or cartographers. Some publishers and packagers employ illustrators (and designers) on short-term contracts. Photography is normally commissioned.

The basis of a book designer's job is visual planning. A designer, operating within technical, cost and time constraints, and taking the views of the editor, and the production and sales departments into account, solves the problem of transforming and enhancing the author's raw material, text and illustrations, to make a printed book that appeals to book buyers and users alike, and legibly and aesthetically conveys its purpose – whether for leisure, information or education. The drawing element of the job usually extends only as far as providing blueprints or rough visuals for others (technical illustrators, artists, typesetters, colour originators or printers) to execute.

Good design standards sell books – whether it is the cover attracting an impulse buyer in a shop or a teacher at an exhibition; the display of a contents page stimulating an academic or professional; the effective use of typography and illustrations conveying mood and excitement or pedagogic aims; or the overall feel bringing pleasure to a giver or collector.

Some publishers, especially in the highly illustrated book (including the high quality book packagers) and art book fields are actively design-led. Their design standards are used as a marketing and sales tool internationally.

Designer's tasks in producing a new title

The point at which a designer is first involved with a new book varies. It may occur before or after the author has completed the manuscript, the designer receiving either an edited or unedited copy. By then the book's overall parameters (e.g. format, extent, illustrations, binding, paper) have been planned by the editor and management.

In some firms editors personally brief designers while in others meetings are organized, attended by the production team and sometimes the sales staff. The outcome is a production specification (part of which determines the budget available for design or illustration services), covering the production methods and proof stages to be used, and the time schedule. It is vital for a designer to be given a clear brief by the editor at the outset. A designer may be able to suggest alternative ideas to save money or to improve sales potential. Assuming the book is not part of a fixed format series or that a pre-existing design cannot be adapted to suit it, the designer's opening tasks are to prepare the type specification and page layout which are supplementary to the book's overall production specification.

Type style specification and page layout grid

The type style specification sets out how the main text, hierarchy of headings and sub-headings, displayed quotations, captions, tables, running heads, page numbers etc. should be typeset in respect of typefaces, sizes, line lengths etc. and of the positioning and spacing of the elements. The page layout is a graphic representation of the printed page – invariably of two facing pages. Layouts are based on a grid – the underlying framework within which text and illustrations are placed on the page. Layout and typographic style considerably affect the readers' perception of a book. The two are interdependent and should, if well designed, allow the author's work to be presented consistently and flexibly, taking into account the aims, character, market, and technical and cost constraints of the book.

Factors affecting their development include the fitting of the author's manuscript into the desired extent; the ability of certain typefaces to cope with mathematics or foreign languages, or to ease reading by early or poor-sighted readers; their suitability for reduction if the book is to be reprinted subsequently in a reduced paperback format; and the typefaces available from a supplier etc.

The designer presents one or more designs in the form of mock-ups to the editorial and production staff for their comments and approval; sometimes typeset or DTP specimen pages are produced.

Typographic mark-up

Once the complete manuscript is edited, the designer carries out the typographic mark-up, that is the addition of typesetting instructions to the manuscript or disk. Some instructions, such as the indication of the heading hierarchy and use of italic or bold within the text, should have been marked in copy-editing. The designer checks, for instance, the editor's hierarchy of headings to ensure they conform to the agreed type specification, and may want them modified. The typesetter follows the specification or style coding. However, depending on the complexity of the material, the designer may indicate the design treatment of recurring text matter which, though covered by the specification, may still need to be marked by using abbreviations or codes. Complex text (including tables) as well as displayed text, such as that of the prelims, may require specific mark-up.

Drawn illustrations

The illustrations may reach the designer before or, more likely, after the author has handed over the manuscript to the publisher. At a much earlier stage, the designer may have briefed the author or supplied the editor with guidelines to help the author prepare drawn illustrations. Designers are usually responsible for commissioning the technical illustrators or artists who execute the final artwork which may be prepared electronically.

When many complex diagrams need to be drawn the designer prepares an artwork specification to serve as a technical reference for illustrators.

Chosen freelance illustrators or artists are contacted directly, or are recruited from artist's agents or commercial studios. The designer, who may have developed or sometimes revisualized the author's roughs, briefs the contact about the purpose of each illustration and the style of execution (including the final appearing size), gives a deadline for completion; the cost is estimated in advance.

The finished artwork returns. The designer checks that the brief has been followed and that the technical standard of the artwork is suitable for processing and reproduction by the printer. Correction cycles follow until all approve. The designer ensures that mistakes attributable to the illustrator are not charged to the publisher.

Proofing stages

With unillustrated books that go straight to page proofs, the edited and marked-up manuscript (together with the type specification and grid) are sent off to the typesetter. But for a book with illustrations grouped on pages, the designer provides a layout. When illustrations are interspersed with the text, the sized artwork and photographs are sent off with the text, or the designer instructs the typesetter to leave specified spaces for the illustrations to be inserted later. During or after the author and editor have read the proofs, the designer fine-tunes the typography and corrects any bad page breaks or layouts.

With illustrated books that go to galley, the designer controls and plans completely the book's layout by means of a manual paste-up or on screen. The designer may be involved with the final selection of photographs and advises whether they will reproduce well. The layout of a page can affect the choice, and the integration of text and illustration influences the sizes of photographs which may be cropped (changing the fixed size of diagrammatic artwork is often too difficult and expensive). The designer tunes the ensuing page proofs and any illustration proofs, spotting visual errors which authors, editors and printers may fail to recognize.

Highly illustrated colour books

The design approach to such books (e.g. adults' and children's general books sold on the quality of their pictorial content; and some low-level textbooks and ELT courses) differs and is closer to that of quality magazine and partwork publishing – the designer's role is more central. Fundamentally, the interrelationship of the word extent and illustrations, and the positioning of colour within the book is planned and controlled, page by page, from the outset and subsequently through numerous proof stages. Specimen pages of selected double-page spreads are produced to aid authors'/contributors'/editors' writing. Moreover, such material (supplemented with the cover and the book dummy) may be used to interest book clubs and/or overseas publishers in co-publication. The designer normally has a greater say over the format, appearance, art direction and creation of the book, which allows more scope to vary its grid and pace, and to provide surprise elements. Some books (including school/ ELT texts) use double-page spreads on topics. The strong headlines, dramatic illustrations and extended captions (often read first) capture the interest of a bookshop browser, mail-order buyer, or pupil.

Books for international co-publication have special design needs. To gain economies in co-printing (i.e. the printing of two or more editions simultaneously), the colour illustrations should remain unaltered in position, whereas the translations of the text are changed on the presses. Thus the typographic design allows for greater length of foreign languages, chosen typefaces have the full range of accents, type running around illustrations is avoided, type is not reversed-out within colour illustrations, and illustrations are not culturally specific to the UK.

Cover design

The cover or jacket protects the book, identifies author/title/ publisher (the ISBN and bar code facilitating ordering), carries the blurb and often the author biography. But its main purpose is to sell. The design should inform as well as attract, be true to the contents, and be tuned to the market. The sales objective of the image is more significant in consumer book publishing (especially critical in mass-market paperback) than other areas because of the importance of retail impulse purchase; and covers are used by the sales department to sell books well in advance of publication to wholesalers and retailers. The image must be powerful enough to attract a browser to pick the book up within a few seconds, and be clear enough to be reproduced in catalogues of the publisher, of a book club, and of overseas publishers or agents.

Printed covers are usually needed three to six months or more ahead of book publication. The designer is briefed at the manuscript editing stage by the commissioning editor and generates rough visuals for approval by the editorial, production and sales departments. The chosen image is developed (and illustrators, photographers, picture researchers commissioned if necessary), the copy typeset, the artwork prepared and proofed. The author may be consulted. Covers arouse strong passions among all participants, and at worst may be revised up to publication.

Skills

Underpinning design is a thorough knowledge of typography and the ways in which books and covers are put together. Designers need perception, clarity of thought, an ability to take a raw manuscript (perhaps badly presented), to analyse it, and come up with an effective design within financial and technical constraints. They should be able to anticipate the problems of readers. It calls for combination of imagination, a knowledge and understanding of current technical processes and DTP software, awareness of the work of leading freelances and of trends and fashions in book design. For cover design a creative mind is preeminent, combined with a gut feeling of what sells.

Designers must develop the ability to extract a brief (tactfully overcoming some editors' quirks and preconceptions) and be able to explain to authors, editors and sales staff (who rarely think in shape, colour and form) how they arrived at a solution, and why it is the best; and they must be able to give clear and unambiguous briefs and instructions to other designers, illustrators, production staff and printers.

Highly illustrated book work requires designers to get under the skin of a subject, to undertake research if necessary, to ask probing questions of experts and to pay due regard to ethnic or cultural sensitivities. The establishment of the all important rapport with in-house staff, illustrators and printers takes time and experience to develop. The handling of artists and illustrators, some of whom can be awkward, calls for a special mixture of tact, pleading or coercion to induce them to produce their best work.

Most designers work on many books simultaneously, all at different stages in production. Thus, like editors, they need to be flexible and self-organizing.

PRODUCTION

The publisher's production department is the link between editors and designers and external suppliers. As the publisher's big spender, it buys the materials and services of the suppliers who manufacture the books. Before a description of that work, there follows a brief summary of the main book production processors provided by firms in the printing industry at home and abroad.

Book production processes

Typesetting and textprocessing

Typesetting is carried out mainly by specialist firms or by printers. Some pundits thought DTP would put such firms out of business but this has not happened. Established firms put aside old equipment and high-priced unionized craft labour, and new firms arose sometimes founded in back bedrooms by former employees, sometimes by computer bureaux. Their core business is textprocessing. They may use DTP systems and/or more powerful systems. They offer a range of services. They re-key manuscripts and enact the typography at very low rates (re-keying is sometimes carried out by out-workers in the UK or in the Third World); translate authors' disks, re-format and correct the inevitable errors; style-code disks supplied, including SGML in selected cases; transfer onerous editorial corrections from the hard-copy to disk; or merely produce the output from fully coded disks supplied. Some firms offer additional editorial and design services while others concentrate on highly technical material or text database management. The vast number of titles with no or minimal illustrations do not require designers to layout the pages – the textprocessors' largely automated pagination systems do it for the publishers. Textprocessors can generally re-key a 100 000 word manuscript and submit page proofs to a publisher within six weeks, much faster if supplied with style-coded disks.

Their laser output devices holding digitized typefaces often use Postscript and are thus like office laser printers. Indeed on non-illustrated books, high resolution office printers may be used. But on illustrated books, textprocessors may output type, line illustrations and photographs to higher resolutions, above 1000 dots per inch (DPI), on to photographic paper (called bromide) or on to film. If the book is mainly not illustrated the paged output is the camera-ready-copy (CRC) from which the book printer makes the printing plates. If the book contains many photographs the paged output is usually on film.

Reproduction of illustrations

Originals of illustrations are converted to film by a 'reproduction (repro) house' or a by a textprocessor or a printer, to sizes specified by the designer.

Book printing presses cannot reproduce directly the continuous shades or tones of grey appearing in monochrome photographs, pencil drawings etc., thus 'the half-tone process' is used. The image of the original is screened, i.e. broken into hundreds of dots of varying size (larger, closer or adjoining dots in dark areas; smaller, further apart, or no dots at all in light areas) which, when printed in black ink only, create the illusion of continuous shades. An electronic scanner digitizes the image and produces the 'screened' film.

In order to print full colour photographs or paintings, the press carries four plates, each inked with one of the basic colours: cyan (a greenish blue); pure yellow; magenta (a purplish red), and black. In combination these produce the illusion of full colour. 'Four-colour printing' dictates that the colour originals be separated into the four basic colours and screened. A scanner produces the four screened films for each illustration.

Various kinds of proofs are submitted to the publisher before the final film of the illustrations is accepted.

Film assembly, imposition and platemaking

The printer assembles the type and illustration films for each printed page; or may be supplied with the CRC from the textprocessor and/or film of illustrations from the repro house. Unified films are produced for every page, and for each colour if necessary. If the text and illustrations are held in digital form they are merged electronically.

Presses do not print one page at a time. Each sheet of paper, printed both sides, carries 8, 16 or 32 pages (or multiples of these), and is eventually folded several times and cut to make a section (or signature) of the book. The printer is responsible for the imposition: the arrangement of the pages that will be printed together on each side of the sheet so that once the sheet is printed and folded the pages will be in the right sequence and position. One large piece of film is made of the imposed pages that will be printed on each side of the sheet. After an ozalid proof check of the film, the printing plates are made from each imposed film. (Unless a quick reprint is expected, the plates are not stored for any length of time.)

Printing

Most books are printed by offset lithography. Lithographic metal plates have a smooth surface which is so treated that the image areas to be printed attract grease (ink) and repel water; and the non-printing areas attract water and repel ink. A plate is clamped around a cylinder on the press, dampened and inked by rollers. The plate rotates against a cylindrical rubber blanket on to which the inked image is offset (printed) and from which the ink is transferred to the paper.

Many rotary offset presses are sheet-fed and vary in plate size and in capabilities: e.g. print only one colour on one side of a sheet during one pass of the paper; print a single colour on each side of the sheet during one pass (perfector machines); print two or four colours on one side during each pass etc. There are also web-fed offset presses that print on to reels, not sheets, of paper. Most mass-market paperbacks are printed on these presses but some are printed on rotary web-fed letterpress presses that carry cylindrical plastic plates on which the areas to be printed stand proud, are inked and impressed directly on to the paper.

Binding and finishing

After printing, the sheets are folded by the printer or possibly by a binding firm. The folded 8, 16 or 32 page sections are collated in sequence to make up every book.

Many hardbacks and some quality paperbacks (including some textbooks) have their sections sewn together. With quality hardbacks, the sewn sections are trimmed on three sides (leaving the sewn spine folds intact), end papers are glued to the first and last sections (unless the text paper is sufficiently strong), any decorative head or tail bands added, strong material glued to the spine to reinforce the hinge with the case, and the spine sometimes rounded. Meanwhile the case is made by gluing the front and back boards (and paper backstrip of the spine) to the 'cloth' which in turn is stamped with title/author/publisher etc. The outer sides of the end papers are pasted, the finished case dropped over the book (spine-side up), and the book squeezed. The jacket (printed on a small colour press, sometimes by another firm) is often laminated with clear plastic film and wraps the finished book. Sometimes the printed cover is glued to the case before binding.

Adhesive binding methods are increasingly used (instead of the more expensive and stronger sewing) for paperbacks and some hardbacks. With 'perfect binding' (used typically for cheap paperbacks) the spine folds of the sections are cut off and the spine edge of the now individual leaves roughened. Glue is applied to hold the leaves together and to stick the printed cover to the book, which is then trimmed on three sides. The cover may have been varnished (on a printing press or special machine) rather than laminated. Other methods, cheaper than sewing but stronger and more expensive than perfect binding, are 'notch' or 'burst' bindings. With these, the spine folds of the sections are not cut off. Instead they are perforated during sheet folding. The perfect binding machine merely injects the glue to hold together the folded sections, applies the cover and trims the book.

The printer/binder packs quantities of the book by shrink wrapping, parcelling or in cartons and delivers them on pallets to the publisher's specified location.

Technical developments

Publishers want to conserve their cash by ordering just sufficient quantities of books to meet expected demand over relatively short periods. If a book is selling well, they need to replenish stock quickly: with mass market paperbacks within one week. Traditional book printing was characterized by much skilled hand work in assembly, imposing the film, and making the plates. There were many stop/start processes. The 'make-ready' on the printing press involved loading the plate and paper, inking the plate and running trial copies to attain quality. On a press which prints 5000 sheets per hour the make-ready consumed a high proportion of the time taken. In the bindery there were free-standing folding and collating machines, lines of women operating sewing machines, guillotines, and men humping paper from one machine to another. But modern printers are capital-intensive. They need to streamline and integrate the process, reduce labour, and have machines turning with the minimum of make-ready time. Advances in the manufacturing of books include greater automation in imposition, electronic output direct to plate, reduction in press machine make-ready time, control of inking by electronic monitoring, and the integration of binding machinery.

However, a completely new approach, high-speed electronic printing, is facilitating the viability of very short-runs. Many publishers face the problem of having to put a book out-of-print because although there is evidence of continuing demand, it is too low to justify the cost of reprinting by conventional methods. For instance, in academic publishing a reprint of under 300 copies to last a year would be difficult. A high-speed, laser-driven electronic printing machine accepts either hard-copy input (which is scanned in) or electronic input of the paged document. It manufactures the copies (or conceivably just a single copy) and binds the document in one operation (one machine, one operator). Such technology is advancing fast and offers the prospect of the printing of a second colour and of full colour on short runs. Thus, on low demand titles, a publisher is given the options of keeping the book in print and reducing stock to the absolute minimum, or of producing versions or updates in small quantities.

Publishers' production departments

Production is closely related to book design. Production staff may design the books or hire freelance designers, or in-house book designers report to the head of production; or there is a separate design department. The production department gives the accounts department information on anticipated costs and their likely timing, details of work in progress, and materials held in stock.

In a small firm an editor may carry out production duties or use freelances or external companies which provide a production service; but with increasing size a firm will employ production specialists. Within a department, there are commonly three main levels of job.

- A production manager/director is responsible for the purchasing policy on sources of supply; establishing standard book sizes and papers; controlling the flow of work and maintaining quality standards; contributing to the preparation of the publishing programme by planning schedules and cost budgets for forthcoming books; and responding to major technical changes such as managing in-house DTP and text coding. This manager contributes to the firm's profitability by buying materials and services at the least possible cost, by conserving the firm's cash by influencing the timing of major items of expenditure and by obtaining the longest possible credit periods from suppliers. The manager also handles the production of certain important books.

- A production controller is responsible for seeing books through the production stages from manuscript to receipt of bound copies. He or she may or may not specialize in part of the list, e.g. illustrated or non-illustrated, technical or non-technical books.

- A production assistant/secretary gives clerical or administrative support to the department by typing, answering the phone, moving proofs around, keeping an eye on the schedules, and telephoning suppliers; and/or by looking after the records, keeping invoices in ledgers and recording production costings etc. Many people start their production careers at this level.

Provisional estimates

The production manager supplies the commissioning editor with provisional estimates of the costs of producing a proposed new title, and may suggest alternative production options. The book is envisaged in broad terms (e.g. format, extent, illustrative content, quality desired, binding style). The estimate summarizes the costs of typesetting, reproduction of any illustrations, printing and binding (inclusive of paper and materials) and enables the costing of different print runs.

Once the author has signed the contract, the manager may advise the author, directly or via the editor, on how the manuscript should be keyed on a wordprocessor so that if appropriate the text can be handled electronically.

Preparing the specification

Once the publisher has accepted the manuscript, a cast-off (a character count of it, or the amount of space it will occupy when set in a given typeface) may be done in the production, design or editorial departments, or by a typesetter. The production controller, who gathers information from the editor or from pre-production meetings, prepares a specification (i.e. a detailed technical description of the book).

The book's desired physical attributes, the amount of money and time available for its production, its destination (home and abroad) and any special market needs (e.g. particular typefaces, a planned reduced format paperback edition or co-edition) are taken into account, and the choice of production processes and of materials is made.

Requesting quotations: print and paper buying

The same clear and unambiguous specification is sent to one or more suppliers who have the right machinery so that they can tender quotations (i.e. a definite price). Although there are printers that carry out all the processes, they may not do all economically or well. Thus, textprocessing, illustration reproduction, and printing/binding specifications may be sent to specialist firms.

A publisher deals with a core of regular and trusted suppliers whose machinery, staff, strengths and weaknesses are known;

but new ones are tried. Sometimes price schedules are negotiated with major print suppliers for standard types of work, which reduces the need for quotations and simplifies estimating. Suppliers may quote discounts on titles processed in batches or during slack periods. Moreover, the long time (e.g. six to eighteen months) books take to produce gives publishers and packagers the option of using overseas suppliers (e.g. in Europe, the Far East or the USA). Most colour book printing now goes abroad. The competitiveness of overseas suppliers vis à vis the UK, is affected greatly by exchange rates, but other factors such as freight and communication costs, longer timescales, and the book's final destination are considered.

Suppliers are assessed on three main criteria: price; quality of work; and service (e.g. ability to keep to dates, or to make up for slippage, and communication). The priority given to each varies by title. For example, a small saving from the cheapest source may be outweighed if that supplier produces inferior work or misses dates.

The quotations are assessed, prices sometimes negotiated downwards and the work awarded. From the quoted prices, another in-house estimate is prepared for management.

Paper is a major cost item and is bought either by the printer, or by the publisher from a paper merchant or directly from a mill. Some publishers store paper as an insurance (against non-availability) for quick reprints, even though that ties up the firm's cash and incurs storage costs.

Scheduling and progressing the book

The controller draws up the time schedule of the internal and external operations that end with the delivery of bound copies to the warehouse a month ahead of the publication date. The schedule, related to those of other books, takes account of any optimum publication date, cashflow demands, the time needed for the tasks and to route material to and from suppliers.

Production staff record progress and chase editors (who chase authors), designers and external suppliers to keep to agreed (or revised) dates. As all the book's material passes between editor and designer, and between publisher and suppliers it is routed via production at every stage, as are editor's and designer's problems with suppliers. Outgoing material is accompanied by documentation and orders, incoming material is logged, and return dates given to editors and designers. If the return dates are not adhered to, the machine time booked at the printers will be missed and the book unduly delayed.

In the more electronically advanced publishers, document management systems track the progress of the material through the production stages.

Monitoring costs and quality

Some books, especially if illustrated, change during production. Deviations from the original estimate and specification (on which the book was judged to be viable) are monitored and costed. Substantial proof corrections quickly erode a title's profitability. Costs incurred to date are recorded and revised estimates of total costs produced, particularly at the page-proof stage. Then the publisher normally fixes the book's retail price and the number to be printed. Suppliers' invoices are checked, queried, or passed for payment.

The controller checks completeness of material at every stage as well as the accuracy of editor's and designer's instructions and the perfection of illustration originals sent to suppliers; and, conversely, the quality of material returned from suppliers. Technical advice is given to editors and designers to help them in their work. Constant contact with suppliers' representatives, and visits to suppliers maintain relationships.

Highly illustrated quality colour books may involve the production manager or controller in approving the first sheets of each section run off the press – whether in the UK or abroad – and taking responsibility for the quality on behalf of the publisher/packager. The printing is compared against the ozalid proof to ensure that corrections have been made, and against the colour proofs.

Advance copies of the bound stock are checked to ensure that the specified materials have been used, and printing and binding are acceptable. Exceptionally if a major error is discovered, an enquiry is held to determine who is to blame and who is to pay. Finally, all the costs of producing the book are compiled.

Other production work

Controllers also cost and organize reprints and new editions; some large publishers employ staff solely for this task. The publisher or packager owning the film does not always use the original printer in which case the film is moved to the new supplier.

Print technologies are changing fast, especially in the application of software and hardware which amalgamates typesetting, digitized illustrations and page make-up. While only some book and journal publishers have in-house DTP and textprocessing, production staff will play an increasingly central role in their introduction.

The printing of editions for other firms (e.g. book clubs, English and foreign language publishers) involves supplying the rights department with estimates of costs. The costs will include printing the bulk order – or if the buyer does the printing, the cost of making duplicate film – and costs of imprint changes – for example, the name of the co-publisher or book club will have to appear on the title page instead of the original publisher's and the details on the copyright page will change; all of this makes a halt in the printing and costs money. When the publisher or packager prints foreign language editions, the overseas publishers supply the typeset film of the translations which is checked by production to ensure it fits the layout of the colour illustrations.

Production staff may also be concerned with the purchasing of the manufacturing of audio and videocassettes, floppy disks, CDs and their special retail or mail-order packaging requirements.

Skills

Fundamental to production is a thorough understanding of current technical processes, of machinery and of materials (their advantages and disadvantages) and, in international buying, of freight systems and methods of payment. (A knowledge of German or French is useful in a department handling international co-editions.) Numeracy, computer literacy skills, the conception of alternative options and the consideration of all components are necessary in costing titles; as are planning and progress chasing skills (e.g. ascertaining and clarifying objectives, setting priorities, assessing strengths and weaknesses of colleagues/suppliers, foreseeing crunch points) to the development of specifications and schedules.

Effective and fluent communication (face-to-face, on the telephone and in writing) with in-house staff and external suppliers is crucial. Production staff must be able to work with editors and designers as a team even though their priorities of tight cost control and the maintenance of dates may conflict with those of editors and designers.

The work is highly administrative, thus requires a good memory, and meticulous attention to detail and record keeping. While friendly working relationships are formed with suppliers, production staff must never get too close to suppliers (otherwise the negotiating edge is lost) and sometimes have to be very tough. They must have the integrity to reject bribes offered by some suppliers.

Production staff come under great pressure. As the buffer between publisher and suppliers they receive kicks from all sides. They must buy competitively, conserve the cash, meet the deadlines, and not make mistakes (which in this area are very expensive to correct). Much time is spent troubleshooting and trying to keep everyone happy. They need to resolve problems, to think laterally and find the best solution, to switch quickly from one thing to another, and thrive under the strain; and to have the constitution of an ox to withstand suppliers' hospitality.

PUBLICITY AND PROMOTION, AND MAIL-ORDER SALES

The aim of this department is to make the media, book trade, and consumers conscious of the company and the wares it offers; and to stimulate demand. The promotional material produced and the interest generated help the sales staff to sell to the book trade (or to schools or colleges) and the rights staff to their customers. Home and overseas customers use the promotional material as a reference source for ordering. Public relations (PR) includes generating free publicity and furthering a company's good image with authors and the media.

The manager of this department usually reports to the marketing/sales director. Many departments consist of just one or two people who do everything, but in medium to large firms there

are usually three levels: manager, publicity or promotion assistants who carry through the publicity/promotion campaigns for
individual books, and secretaries/assistants.

Staff in large publishing groups may be attached to particular
firms or imprints in the group, concerned with adult or children's
publishing; or with educational, ELT, academic, or professional
book publishing etc. The work may be divided by task. In some
consumer book publishers, specialists deal solely with public
relations, or with the development of promotional and point-of-
sale (POS) material and catalogues, or with space advertising or
copywriting; or in some academic and professional book publishers with textbooks, mail-order sales or journal promotion.
Publishers of all kinds also hire advertising agencies (especially
for major projects or authors), freelance publicists, direct mail
specialists etc. While in-house designers and production staff are
sometimes used, publicity and promotion staff may commission
freelance designers and buy print themselves because these suppliers are not those producing the books.

Publicity and promotion encompass numerous, diverse activities. The publicity manager may first become involved at the
publishing proposal stage or immediately post-contract. From
discussions with editors and sales staff, each book is evaluated
and decisions made on the promotional material (and any
advertisements) required, and what publicity and media coverage might be sought. The (usually small) promotion budget set
may be proportional to the expected sales revenue. It is impossible to promote all books equally and, especially in consumer
book publishing, the lead titles receive by far the largest budgets.
The key judgement on every title lies in deciding how much to
spend to generate profitable sales that more than recoup the
outlay.

Before a review of specific techniques, a basic strategy used
on most new books follows.

A basic promotion strategy

Around manuscript delivery, the author completes a question-
naire. It returns via the editor. The author supplies personal
information, a biography, a blurb, a short synopsis, the book's
main selling points and intended readership or applicability to

courses, lists of print and broadcast media (and individuals) that might review or publicize the book etc.

Advance information sheet

The promotion assistant prepares the book's advance information sheet (AIS) which contains bibliographic information (e.g. title, author, format, extent, illustrative content, hardback/paperback, ISBN, planned price and publication date); synopsis/blurb/contents; main selling points, market profile; author biography etc. It is mailed, say, three to nine months ahead of publication to all the people who help sell the book: the publisher's sales force and overseas agents, booksellers, wholesalers, and library suppliers etc. Wholesalers and library suppliers need the information (at least three months in advance) to enter the title in their catalogues to secure advance orders.

Cover

The cover is another promotional item used by the publisher's home and export sales departments, some library suppliers and overseas agents. It is produced preferably well ahead of publication. The cover blurb is written or re-written by the editor, by the promotion assistant, or by an in-house or freelance copywriter.

Catalogues

Catalogue preparation is a major task: it involves an assistant in gathering information from all round the firm, updating it, collecting illustrations, copywriting, briefing a designer, sometimes print buying, and carrying through all the production stages.

The twin aims of catalogues are to present the firm and its products attractively so that buyers (the book trade and consumers) select its wares; and to act as an informative, readily understandable and accurate reference so that products can be ordered easily through the supply chain at home and abroad.

Consumer book publishers normally produce catalogues announcing their forthcoming books geared to their six monthly marketing/selling cycles, the autumn/winter catalogue appearing in time for the preceding mid-summer sales conference, the spring/summer catalogue appearing for the preceding Christmas sales conference. Mass-market paperback publishers typically issue monthly catalogues or stocklists about three months ahead of the publication month covered. Catalogues are distributed to all members of the supply chain and to main libraries, to the public (e.g. via booksellers to account customers), and to review editors and the media. The stocklists covering new and backlist books which accompany catalogues are used by the publisher's reps and the book trade for ordering.

Educational, academic, STM and professional publishers usually arrange their catalogues by subject or by groups of allied subjects. Different subject catalogues may be produced for different levels of the education system and books within a textbook catalogue (which includes selected backlist) may be arranged or classified by the age group, or examination or academic level served. Catalogues are produced annually to cover the following year's publications, or six-monthly or more frequently. Although the catalogues are mailed to selected booksellers, they are aimed primarily at teachers/academics/professionals – those who decide to purchase or adopt the books – and are distributed to schools or academic libraries, institutions, departments (and where appropriate to targeted subject specialists or professionals, and to industry).

Publishers also produce, say annually, complete catalogues containing summary information on all new and backlist titles. As the main reference source of the publisher's output, it is used by the book trade, libraries and others at home and overseas.

Bibliographies

Giving the main bibliographers accurate information on each title at the right time is essential and promotes the book worldwide cheaply. For example, information given to Whitaker at least three months ahead of publication lists the title in *The Bookseller*, and other bibliographies, including Whitaker's *Books in Print* and *Bookbank* on CD-ROM. These alert booksellers to new titles, enable them to trace backlist titles and facilitate ordering. The statutory obligation to send six gratis copies to the copyright libraries, ensures that the title is listed in the weekly additions to the *British National Bibliography* (BNB) and alerts the libraries. The advantage of sending the British Library information earlier so that they can prepare the Cataloguing in Publication (CIP) entry is that the book is listed in the BNB sooner (especially important for academic and STM titles).

Reviews

Once bound copies are received, a review list is prepared, tailor-made for the title, taking account of the author's ideas and contacts. The review copies are sent out with a review slip which details the title, author, price, binding, ISBN and publication date, and requests a review. Any reviews received are circulated in-house and to the author.

Technical developments

DTP is widely adopted in the preparation of promotional material and catalogues. However, some publishers build data-bases containing coded information on their new and backlist titles. Such information includes bibliographic details as well as sales copy of different lengths and review responses etc. It allows them to retrieve and manipulate information about their books and other products in a form most suited to their customers. The output may be printed, or transmitted electronically to customers and to information providers such as librarians, bibliographers and wholesalers.

The publishers which emphasize direct-mail promotion and mail-order selling, especially the educational, academic, STM and professional book publishers, marshal in-coming information in order to define customer's buying patterns and needs, which in turn guides the out-flow of information and the promotional effort.

Additional publicity and promotion techniques

Free publicity and public relations

Engineering free publicity in the print and broadcast media is more important in consumer book publishing than in any other, and spreads word-of-mouth knowledge about the book. The publicist is in constant contact with press and magazine editors, journalists, radio and television producers. With so many books and authors competing for media space, a book or author (especially a fiction writer) has to be carefully positioned in the market place. At the manuscript stage, the publicist targets the market, and formulates a publicity plan. A key part of the task is identifying the appropriate media (e.g. particular newspapers and magazines, programmes) that would be interested and helping them make their decisions. Book publicity departments are in effect extensions of the media and the media become part of the PR machine. The stimulated coverage should occur around publication. Coverage is gained from features, author promotions (e.g. tours, signing sessions, radio and television appearances), press releases, parties etc. Signing sessions, competitions for booksellers, and joint promotions with booksellers are arranged in close conjunction with the sales department. Sales staff are warned about any impending coverage so that they can inform the booksellers who are thus more likely to stock the book which in turns sells more copies.

Other publicity involves informing the trade press about the firm, distributing bound proof copies to influential people, entering titles for literary prizes, helping to plan and attend exhibitions (including the publisher's own sales conferences), maintaining contact with The Publishers Association, the Book Trust and the British Council (all of which promote books) and sometimes answering queries from the public, teachers, librarians and booksellers.

Serial rights

In consumer book publishing, publicity staff instead of the rights department may sell serial rights to their contacts in the press and magazines. Extracts or serials should appear around book publication and produce income and publicity.

Point-of-sale material

Eye-catching material (e.g. posters, display kits, copy holders, dumpbins, brochures, badges etc.) is designed to focus booksellers' and readers' attention on major books, series or brand imprints; to make shops more enticing; and to capture display space, at home and abroad. Produced mainly for consumer books (but sometimes for major reference books and textbooks), most is declined or thrown away by booksellers. Nevertheless, it shows the publisher's commitment to the book and assists advance selling to the book trade and customers abroad.

A publisher may provide major retailers with spinners or special shelving to display its books, though competitors' titles may creep in.

Media advertising

For most books, the high cost of advertising in the press, magazines, or on television or radio, or by poster would not be recouped by the sales generated. Thus it is used very selectively, and short-lived large-scale consumer advertising is restricted to major consumer books, revision aids and reference books etc. Although its effectiveness is intangible, it encourages the book trade to buy and display the book and pleases authors and agents. Consumer book publishers also advertise to the book trade in *The Bookseller* or *Publishing News* – any advertisement appearing two to four months ahead of book publication so that the sales force has time to back it up.

The non-consumer book publishers advertise very selectively in specialist magazines, and journals – ostensibly to sell books, but also to please authors and attract new ones.

The main tasks involved in advertising are conceiving selling ideas from editorial concepts, relating advertising to the other promotions, copywriting and visualizing with a designer, media planning, negotiating the best rates and positions, and maintaining tight budgetary control.

Direct mail promotion

The preparation and mailing of brochures or leaflets advertising a major title, or allied titles, direct to targeted specialist audiences at their place of work forms a large part of the work of promotion assistants in educational, academic, STM and professional book and journal publishers. Together with mailed subject catalogues (and to some extent reviews) it is the main promotional means by which teachers/academics/professionals and librarians learn about new titles and (for textbooks and journals) about backlist titles (monographs are normally promoted only once). Together with the editor, the promotion assistant works out the scope of the market, the best approach, what kind of mailing piece is appropriate, the time it should be distributed and to whom, i.e. which mailing list to use, within the allocated budget.

The assistant writes the copy, often designs it, and carries through the production stages. While some publishers keep their own mailing lists, lists are selected and rented from specialist mailing houses which may distribute the material. Depending on the export arrangements, material may be mailed direct to libraries, teachers, academics and booksellers in selected countries.

Textbook inspection copy service

Teachers and academics are unlikely to prescribe a book for student use unless they have examined a copy first. Titles (e.g. textbooks and children's books) that are expected to be ordered in bulk for schools or placed on a reading list of books which students should buy (excluding monographs and professional reference titles) are marked on catalogues/leaflets, which contain inspection copy order forms. The teacher, having placed the order, completes a reply card (enclosed with the book) which asks for comments on the suitability of the book; and if the book is adopted, the number of students on the course and the name of the supplier. If adopted, the recipient keeps the book free; if not, pays for it or returns it. The results and response rates are used for market research. In tertiary publishing the information is passed to the sales staff who alert the booksellers through which the books are purchased. In school textbook publishing the UK schools ordering class sets directly are recorded. Textbook publishers of all levels build databases of adoptions (e.g. institution, course, student numbers) for subsequent follow-up and targeting.

Some publishers send free copies of textbooks to influential teachers.

Mail-order sales and direct marketing

Most books are sold via booksellers to end users. Some booksellers, especially the specialist, sell by mail order and may produce catalogues. The book clubs (general interest and specialist) supply by mail order about ten per cent of publishers' sales, mainly consumer books. But some publishers sell a proportion of their books direct to end-users.

At one extreme, there are the few main mail-order firms which publish a small number of highly illustrated information books or series, or condensed fiction in enormous quantities for UK households. At the other, are firms which publish high-priced reference/loose-leaf works for defined professional markets (e.g. legal, accountancy, finance, business), to people who may not visit bookshops. In between, some of the academic and STM book publishers increasingly solicit orders from academics/scientists/professionals to supplement their main sales through bookshops. Consumer book publishers rarely solicit direct orders overtly, because most are unable to identify readers and addresses, and the price of many of their books is pitched at retail outlets and is too low to make it cost-effective.

The greater a publisher's reliance on bookshop sales, the greater the pressure from booksellers against the publisher's use of direct marketing: some booksellers believe it erodes their business. Publishers thus adopt different attitudes to its use. However, paradoxically, it leads to increased sales (the echo effect) through booksellers or library suppliers – people or organizations who are prompted to buy then order through the conventional channels.

The direct marketing vehicle may be a space advertisement, an insert in a magazine or book, or a mailed item (a catalogue or leaflet and personalized letter). Whatever the means, the promotion assistant encourages direct purchase (sometimes by special offers) and includes a response facility which eases ordering and payment (e.g. by freepost, telephone, fax and credit card). By assessing the response rates, direct marketing allows the statistical testing of the effectiveness of different offers and creative approaches (such as the design of the envelope, letter and leaflet), their timing and frequency, and of the vehicle.

The main vehicle is usually direct mail – the extension of direct mail promotion described above – giving much space for the message at little extra cost. The mailing list (ideally up-to-date, accurate and appropriate for the product) is of prime importance. List brokers may be used, lists are rented or acquired free, and are tested initially. Lists may be gathered from firms which specialize in constructing lists in educational, academic and professional areas, from associations, journal subscribers, conference delegates etc. and from authors. In time the best lists are the publisher's own, built from successive sales. Sometimes they are rented from, or to, other publishers. The most likely customers are targeted regularly with the most appropriate titles, and varying amounts are spent to acquire and keep different levels of customer.

Direct marketing sells books quickly (most feedback is usually in weeks, not many months) and a response rate of 1 or 2 per cent would be thought a success, though rates of up to 5, 10 or 15 per cent plus are possible. But if poorly executed much money can be lost even though the books are sold at full price or at modest discount.

Telemarketing, by a publisher's own staff or by a retained agency, is sometimes used to follow up a mailshot, for example, to reach teachers and professionals at their place of work. However, it plays a relatively minor part in the marketing mix. The use of fax marketing and of on-line academic networks are further avenues.

Export promotion

The promotional items (catalogues, leaflets, POS material) are distributed abroad, usually unaltered, but may be prepared especially for overseas agents and booksellers, such as in ELT, academic/STM and professional fields.

Children's publishing

Children's books, reaching a general retail market, libraries and schools, combine the techniques of general and educational publishing. The publicist creates and mails the catalogues etc. (distributed to the book trade, schools and libraries), generates free publicity (e.g. author promotions during Children's Book Week), organizes exhibitions, attends conferences and liaises with schools and libraries; and, unusually, may dress up as a large, ungainly creature for a delighted audience.

Skills

Overall, an interest in the firm's books and the ability to identify the editorial reasoning and sales potential is necessary. Creativity is needed in originating ideas for promoting a wide range of titles, as well as an understanding of the relationships between costs and expected sales in maximizing the profit potential of each title, within budget.

Good personal relations inside the company (particularly with editors) and outside the company are vital, as are administrative and planning skills.

The development of promotional material engages copywriting (which can be learnt by literate people who appreciate the different styles demanded for different lists and books), editorial, production and DTP skills. In direct mail promotion or selling an assistant acts like a detective (working out where the people are and how to reach them). Public relations' work involves living on one's wits, exchanging favours with the media, establishing a rapport and trust with all kinds of media and authors, knowing when to hype and when to hold back, being able to talk oneself in and out of situations fast, having supreme self-confidence and a high tolerance of rude people and working anti-social hours.

HOME SALES

Although promotion staff stimulate demand, it is the sales staff who realize the income by sustained face-to-face selling to the buyers of the intermediary firms (in textbook publishing they promote and sell books to teachers).

The marketing/sales director, usually supported by a home sales manager, plans and organizes the sales effort. The sales management comments on editors' new book or edition proposals (e.g. sales forecasting and pricing), and is involved with reprinting and re-pricing decisions, and with the disposal of overstocks by remaindering or pulping.

Broadly speaking, publishers derive most of their sales revenue from a small number of customers, and small revenue from a great number. Typically 20% of customers account for 80% of sales. In consumer book publishing, especially, the bookselling chains dominate, followed by wholesalers and library suppliers.

The sales manager sells titles say three or more months ahead of publication to the buyers of such key (or house) accounts, and discusses the publisher's and the large retailers' promotion plans. Although some chains delegate purchasing decisions to branch buyers who are called on by publishers' sales representatives (reps), others (including the largest) buy centrally and relate order quantities to the sizes and character of their branches. Chains adopting strong central buying preclude visits by reps, which has reduced the number of reps. CTN's, drug and department stores, supermarkets etc., serviced exclusively by the wholesale merchandisers or supplied directly by publishers, buy centrally.

A 'special sales' manager may also sell to non-book wholesalers, major non-book retailers, and sometimes to remainder or promotion book imprints and book clubs. Highly illustrated own-brand titles may be sold to supermarket chains. Premium sales, where the book is given away with a product or service, may be made.

Publishers sell books to customers on the following terms (definitions of which vary). On firm orders the bookseller agrees to accept the books, to pay for them (preferably on one month's credit, unless otherwise agreed) and not to return them for credit without prior permission from the publisher, usually from the rep or the sales manager. The bookseller takes the risk that the books may not sell and that the publisher may sometimes refuse returns. Powerful booksellers may thus either request a higher discount and/or be more cautious on the quantity ordered.

Under the following terms the bookseller takes less risk. On see safe orders, the bookseller can within a specified period return books (provided that they are in saleable condition) for credit, or in exchange for other books. The bookseller's account is charged at the time of supply, and payment is due at the expiry of credit. Publishers prefer see safe to sale or return, on which the bookseller within a specified period can return books and no charge will be raised. Payment is not usually due until the end of the specified period, or the books are sold. In each instance the bookseller pays for the return carriage, unless otherwise agreed.

Sometimes an individual large order for a new book placed by a branch book buyer or an independent bookseller may in part be firm, the remainder bought see safe. The terms of trade between publishers and their customers and their effect on discounts, credit periods and levels of returns are in a state of flux.

In medium to large publishers a home sales manager (supported by office staff) runs the sales force. Small publishers cannot afford the high cost of their own reps and so either have their lists sold by a larger firm, or use freelances who are paid a commission (say 10 per cent on net receipts from sales). But preferably a publisher employs its own full-time reps. Each rep covers a discrete area (a territory), is supplied with a car, receives expenses and a salary. Some publishers, more often consumer book firms, pay reps bonuses for exceeding sales targets. The reps, who usually live in their territories, meet together with the in-house staff (e.g. senior managers, editors and publicity staff) only at the sales conferences (two to four times per year), where they learn about the new books, promotional plans and priorities. Following the manager's instructions (about such things as frequency of visits to customers), the reps manage their areas. They are sent all the promotion material (advance information sheets, jackets/covers etc.) and feedback orders and reports on their activities, and on the response of customers.

Consumer book publishers' reps

The large consumer book publishers may have several sales forces specializing in particular, or groups of imprints.

Each rep keeps a file on customers, listing their interests, opening hours etc. They visit mainly booksellers (the branches of the chains and the independents), any wholesalers or library suppliers within their areas, and other outlets which justify the high cost of calling. The reps prepare their own folders with clear plastic sleeves containing neatly placed covers, and other information to show buyers. The folder contains the covers of forthcoming books over, for instance, the following two, three or more months, and the lead titles are usually at the front. They use the folder as a visual aid to sell books on subscription (in advance), and the catalogue for covering the backlist. They rarely carry finished copies, apart from exceptions such as children's illustrated books.

The reps work out their own journeys, taking account of the sales manager's instructions. Retailers are graded by importance:

the small number of large bookshops receive the most frequent visits (e.g. weekly/fortnightly/monthly); others receive regular visits (e.g. quarterly); whereas small ones are seen only occasionally (e.g. six monthly). (Small bookshops ordering insufficient copies are omitted).

In addition to their daily selling, reps discuss with customers, especially with the major booksellers, the latter's promotional plans for the year and the availability of a publisher's own promotional in-store support (such as POS material and authors' presence). Reps usually make appointments with buyers and sometimes send them the current stocklist. The following example gives an impression of a rep's visit to a bookshop.

A rep's aim is to obtain advance orders on forthcoming books from all the main bookshops in time for the stock to be delivered before publication. If the buyers make out the orders instead of reps, the reps want the orders to be sent direct to their publishers, not via higher discount wholesalers. During a call they will cover the new books to be published in a certain period and take up the new books from that point in a subsequent visit. However, small and infrequently visited bookshops may be sold new books post-publication.

The meeting with the buyer takes place in an office or across the counter. The first few minutes are spent discussing trade gossip and the shop. Reps provide the main contact between booksellers and publishers, and should be able to supply the most recent information on all the firm's titles.

The rep usually leads off with a major, strongly promoted title. The prime aim is to put the buyer in a positive buying frame of mind. Two to three minutes are spent in presenting a lead title. Showing the cover, the rep talks about the book and author, covering such aspects as its contents, what part of the market it is aimed at, why it is good, and sometimes the competition, previous books by the author, and the promotion. Although more time is devoted to the main titles, the rep generally has under a minute per title, just one or two sentences, to sell it. If the book is of local interest or is going to receive publicity, this is mentioned. Reps keep records of orders, so that they can remind buyers of orders placed on authors' previous books.

Some publishers provide their reps with lap-top computers which allow them to provide current information on stock availability, order status, sales history etc. and to download information, such as orders, back to their publishers through their home or hotel telephone that evening.

To avoid diluting the buyer's interest the rep, aware of his or her buying pattern, concentrates on those titles likely to sell in that particular shop (retailers' customer profiles differ greatly). The running order for presenting books varies: e.g. the rep may keep a fairly attractive title near to the end to stimulate a buyer's waning interest. But if the buyer is on edge, the rep may bring forward all the stronger titles, and try the weaker ones at the end. The actual total selling time may take only ten to fifteen minutes, but it may last well over the hour if the rep has many exciting books or if the buyer and rep are friends. Large shops with departmental buyers can take all morning.

There is a common understanding between an experienced rep and a good buyer with regard to the titles and order quantities that can be sold in that particular shop. Weak buyers need help. A good buyer is often aware of the books before the rep calls and can estimate within a few seconds the number of sales. But a buyer may want a larger quantity than the rep had in mind or conversely an order which the rep feels too low. Knowing that the book is selling well elsewhere or sensing that the buyer does not appreciate some aspect, the rep mentions that and suggests a higher quantity. If the rep is trusted, the buyer may increase the order. Part of the persuasion may involve the rep in allowing greater freedom on returns within the firm's overall policy.

While there are bookshops which expect reps to do their stock checking and re-ordering for them, booksellers' electronic stock control systems should override their intervention. Even so, reps may tactfully remind buyers of titles missing from the shelves or mention a title that is gaining media attention etc.

Other aspects of the reps' visits include the following: backed up by attractive POS material, the rep tries to persuade the bookseller to mount special window or instore displays offering incentive terms if necessary. The bookseller may ask the rep to arrange an author signing session in the shop. The rep reports back to the publisher's sales manager to see whether it is feasible. Reps also feed back promotion ideas used by other publishers which could be emulated; and occasionally reps make editorial suggestions. They may also debt chase.

Paperback forces

Some of the major mass-market paperback houses (which also have trade paperback lists) retain separate sales forces who visit a greater range of retailers more frequently, such as twice weekly or weekly, to meet the demands of the faster stock turnover. They may also cover regional paperback wholesalers.

Paperback reps tend to make more calls per day of shorter duration and may win subscriptions for many titles in a matter of seconds. Booksellers must order a minimum quantity (e.g. 20–30 assorted copies) but the returns policy is far freer. Reps sometimes stock the shelves devoted to their house.

Publishers with extensive, fast-selling and complex backlists may retain 'stock-checking merchandisers' who visit major city centre and airport bookshops. They check the stock, and the store buyer either orders stock up to a previously agreed level or agrees the order with the publisher's rep who calls the next day. Some publishers use 'planagrams' whereby the buyer and rep or merchandiser manage stock within agreed display units, such as spinners, devoted solely to the publisher's books.

Academic and STM reps

The sales forces (smaller than those of consumer book publishers) visit a limited range of bookshops which stock their titles, and may call on specialist mail-order booksellers and library suppliers which supply books to home and export markets.

Additionally they may visit campuses in order to identify courses and the lecturers who take the textbook recommendation decisions. While to a limited extent they encourage academics to order personally, or through their library, monographs and reference books (and sometimes journals and software), their main thrust is to secure textbook adoptions. Using the promotional material and occasionally bound copies, they present the most relevant texts to individual lecturers who, if interested, are sent inspection copies. The rep, apart from supplying general information on the firm to academics, also undertakes market research such as looking at reading lists to check new and old adoptions or recommendations, and discussing with lecturers trends in subjects generally and particularly in relation to the firm's and competitors' titles. Sometimes they pick up new ideas and potential authors, to be developed by editors.

There is a great disparity among publishers regarding the proportion of the reps' time spent visiting booksellers and campuses. Many firms rely on direct mail promotion and reps devote most time to booksellers, whereas the reps of the American-founded scientific and technical publishers, and some of the large UK textbook publishers emphasize college calling. Owing to the difficulty of combining bookseller and college calling cycles, they may separate the activity. The college reps aim to see say 15 lecturers per day, about 4000 over the year.

When visiting bookshops, a main task is to ensure that adopted texts are stocked in good time, in the right quantities. The busiest time of college-related shops (which derive say 70% of sales from five months of the year) is from the start of the academic year through to Christmas, followed by a secondary peak in the New Year to serve semester course starts. Thus the rep's key period, from mid-summer onwards, is the run-up to October. Although good booksellers forge links with lecturers and solicit reading lists around May, reps alert buyers to adoptions from information gathered from campus visits and from inspection copy reply cards. Reluctant buyers are eventually triggered into building up their stock by the students. Only a small number of booksellers stock monographs and very high priced reference books; such books are supplied by bookshops in response to orders. However academic reps also sell titles more dependent on retail exposure and lacking a safety net. With these a crucial aim is to get bookshops to stock and display the books, otherwise sales are lost. Booksellers are encouraged to distribute the promotional material and to mount special displays. Another activity is setting up and attending exhibitions at academic conferences. Large firms employ full-time staff solely for UK and European conferences.

Educational reps

School publishers employ full-time educational reps supplemented with term-time reps (often parents or ex-teachers) managed by the full-timers. The large publishers have separate sales forces covering primary and secondary schools, and possibly the further education sector. Additionally, they may appoint specialist advisers (ex-teachers) in the major subject areas. They provide product training for reps, give talks to teachers and promote to local advisers. A rep of a large company may cover just two counties while one in a small company may have to cover a whole region.

During term time reps usually visit two to three secondary schools per day or up to five primary schools. Large primary schools warrant coverage similar to a secondary school. The number of schools visited per day is related to their proximity.

Educational publishers usually hold two or three sales conferences a year (before the opening of terms), at which the commissioning editors present the new books. The marketing/sales manager directs the priorities. The reps relate what they are told at the centre to their particular areas and schools. Conferences enable the reps to report on sales, and on the response from their schools.

The key period and busiest time for reps is the spring term when teachers select what they will use for the next school year (authorities' capitation begins 1 April). The summer term is quieter though there is quite a lot of pick-up work. The winter term becomes progressively more important towards its end.

Educational reps carry heavy cases of books (sometimes several hundred titles), and the promotional material, including advance information on forthcoming titles. A rep sets up the exhibition of books (arranged on the shelves formed by the open cases) usually in the staffroom, or, sometimes less satisfactory, in the library or marking room. The idea is to catch the eye of teachers as they come in for morning coffee or lunchtime breaks or have a free period. The aim is to make sure that the people who influence or determine the choice of teaching material used are aware of what is available; that they know the key aspects of the books displayed. The rep can then decide what inspection copies should be sent and to whom. In small primary schools, headteachers usually choose the materials to be used; in secondary schools and large primary schools departmental heads have the most influence. Thus a rep will try and see them, sometimes by appointment to talk about forthcoming titles, but mainly to show them finished copies. Teachers are asked what they are using and whether they are satisfied. If it is a competitor's book and there is a sign of hesitation, this provides an opening for a rep to discuss the merits of his or her books. Experienced reps know the content not only of their own books but of their competitor's too, and recount the experience of teachers in other schools. If a teacher shows sufficient interest a rep will ask for an inspection copy to be sent. Occasionally copies of key books are left behind. Although priority is given to new books, especially those introducing a comprehensive course of study for National Curriculum core subjects, the promotion of the backlist is vital. In those schools which manage their own budgets, reps encourage direct orders to the publisher, offering incentive discounts on sizeable quantities if necessary.

Market research includes the regular feedback of information such as teachers' suggestions, the response of teachers to their own and competitors' books, information on competitors' books, buying policies, local authority guidelines affecting purchases, and gaps in the market. Sometimes reps suggest ideas for books to the commissioning editors, give advice to teachers who are considering authorship and discover new authors.

Apart from visiting schools, reps ensure that their books are included in reference collections, maintain contact with inspectors and local authority advisers, and sometimes conduct seminars. They are also involved in setting up and staffing local exhibitions, and the major exhibitions linked to national subject conferences held in vacations. Generally speaking, however, reps who work long hours during term time, benefit from the school holidays.

Skills

Common features of all good reps are their energy, self-motivation and discipline which gets them out of bed very early, and makes them work long hours, and withstand the physical ardours of driving and carrying heavy bags. They should have clean driving licences. Being alone, reps need to be well-organized to keep up with the paperwork and very good organizers of their own time.

A good trade rep knows the books and the customers' businesses, interests and systems, calls repeatedly and regularly with good warning, appears on time, introduces the books well, succinctly and enthusiastically, gains the buyer's confidence and trust, gets the order and is welcomed back. Although reps are given priorities, their skill is to determine which books are best for their area and each outlet, and what size of orders are suitable. They gain the confidence of buyers by recommending books that prove themselves.

On meeting buyers reps need to be alert and make a good first impression. Listening and watching they adjust their selling style and procedure to a buyer's character and mood. They need to be flexible, pitching their style within a range from soft to hard sell, and sense when to talk and when not to. A rep is part amateur psychologist, part actor. Both buyers and sales managers want reps to present their firms honestly, to be diplomatic and have authority. When a buyer asks for special terms or wants to return books, or some other favour, a rep must be able to make decisions which are best for the company but at the same time good for the customer.

Educational and college reps must have a lively interest in education and ability to get on well with the kind of people in those professions. Overt hard selling is inappropriate. Rather a rep (who needs to be fully conversant with all the important changes in approach and course content in the main subject areas) needs to be able to talk about the problems faced by teachers, the kinds of materials used, and the ways a teacher likes to use them, and then has to be able to suggest and promote a suitable book.

EXPORT SALES

There are various ways of organizing export sales staff within a publishing house. In small firms the sales director may be responsible for home sales and for export arrangements, spending perhaps one or two months abroad annually. In larger firms there are separate export departments headed by an export sales manager (the counterpart of the home sales manager) who may report to the sales/marketing director. An export manager may be supported by an assistant and a secretary. In still larger firms (often the major publishing groups) there may be an export director in charge of staff such as regional sales executives or area export managers who look after all the group's lists in specific areas of the world, or are possibly concerned with particular lists of the group. They are usually responsible for all export sales within their designated areas and for the arrangements made with various kinds of overseas agents. Their direct selling may also extend to bookshops. A characteristic of all these export specialists is that they are usually expected to spend anything from three to six months abroad annually. Medium and large publishers may employ British export sales representatives who may cover parts or the whole of Europe or other areas of the world. Generally speaking, the larger the company the smaller the geographical area covered by each representative; but compared to the home market their territories are vast (e.g. one or more countries) and their calls to importing book trade customers far less frequent. They are either home-based, travelling abroad for up to six months annually, or resident overseas. Some of the major publishing groups station UK nationals in small offices in countries outside the fields of operation of their overseas firms. They are mainly concerned with promoting the firm's books, liaising with and supervising arrangements made with local distributors, opening up the market, and when appropriate employing local representatives. The export-orientated ELT divisions of major publishers typically have their own export sections deploying any of the above methods. Publishers may also employ full-time local nationals in some areas to represent their interests.

The staff numbers of UK export departments are paradoxically far smaller than the home sales side because much of the work of promoting and selling books is carried out abroad. The main export arrangements are as follows.

Main export arrangements and terms of sale

- In countries where there are firms connected through ownership with the UK publisher, such firms usually have the exclusive right to publish the UK firm's output. Nevertheless, certain UK titles may be licensed to, or distributed by, other firms.
- Within a territory (e.g. a country) a stockholding agent usually has the exclusive distribution rights for part of, or the whole of, the publisher's output – the market is closed. The agent services the orders originating from

customers within the territory and collects the money. Normally, but not always the agent carries out the promotion and sales representation as well. Such agents may be wholesalers/booksellers, importers or branches of other UK publishers. Sometimes, exclusivity is restricted to part of the publisher's output or important named customers within the territory deal directly with the publisher – the market is semi-closed.

- In the open market – countries outside the closed markets of the exclusive stockholding agents (and of the publisher's overseas firms) – the publisher deals directly with the local book trade. However, non-exclusive distribution arrangements may be made with certain local 'preferential' stockists (e.g. wholesalers) which receive more favourable terms from the publisher. The local booksellers can order either directly from the publisher or from the stockist. Some stockists also promote and sales-represent the publisher's books.

- Independent reps or firms ('bag carrying agents') are appointed to promote and sales-represent the books in specified countries – usually but not always in open markets. Carrying many publishers' lists, they are based in the UK or abroad. They receive a commission on net sales revenue from the territory. On mainland Europe, especially, such reps face a loss of commission on orders sent by booksellers to UK exporting wholesalers instead of via the rep or direct to their publisher.

The agents, wholesalers and booksellers trading in the books receive discounts, usually off the UK published price, and normally higher than home discounts, from the publisher. They then add their costs and profit which results in book prices being higher than those in the UK. Compared to the UK, customers' credit periods are longer (e.g. 90 days from date of invoice) but can extend to six months or more from slow-paying parts of the world. Wherever possible 'firm sales' are made, though some unsold books are returned (especially general paperbacks).

Commonly, the books are supplied 'Ex-warehouse' – the customer bears the cost from the publisher's (or printer's) door; or

'Free on Board' (FOB) – the publisher delivers the books free to the buyer's appointed UK shipping agent (buyers within a country may co-ordinate and nominate a UK export consolidator for economy). However, some books may be supplied 'Cost, Insurance and Freight' (CIF) – the publisher bears all the costs up to their arrival in a port or town. In return for saving the customer cost and (if the goods are sent air freight) time, the discount and credit period may be cut back. Sometimes bulk stocks are supplied 'on consignment': the customer pays only on sales made and has the right to return unsolds.

Other export sales not under the control of the publisher are made by the UK export wholesalers/booksellers/library suppliers. The largest are internationally based and promote, sell and distribute books worldwide (such firms are major 'home' customers of academic and STM publishers). And end-users seeking the cheapest source of supply (especially libraries) 'buy round' the publishers' arrangements by ordering books from library suppliers, US exporters, wholesalers etc. which ignore exclusive territorial markets.

The information flow and personal selling

Communication with the international network is vital. People abroad must be persuaded to concentrate on promoting and selling the firm's titles rather than those of others. Constant contact takes the form of the supply of information, fax, telephone calls and overseas visits.

The export sales manager who initially provides market intelligence and sales forecasts to editors (taking account of any excluded territories), participates in discussions regarding any competing overseas rights sales and selects titles that, it is anticipated, will generate the major part of new book export turnover: they will receive the most emphasis abroad generally, or specifically in particular markets.

The advance information sheets, catalogues, leaflets, jackets/covers, point-of-sale material cascade on to the agents and representatives who use that material to publicize the publisher's titles within their markets. (Some agents prepare their own catalogues from information supplied, while others send out UK originated material.) Agents may generate free media publicity, secure reviews, mail catalogues, sometimes place advertisements, attend exhibitions and operate a textbook inspection copy service.

The UK publisher too may mail promotional material direct to, for example, wholesalers, booksellers, libraries, British Council offices, academics and professionals, send books for review to learned journals, send complimentary copies of textbooks to influential people and operate an inspection copy service from the UK. The promotion efforts of publisher and agent may overlap.

Of equal importance is the quality and regularity of the response from agents and representatives who provide general feedback on their activities and on market conditions, and specific feedback on individual titles (such as requests for more material).

Overwhelmingly, however, export sales are generated by personal selling. The senior export staff give presentations to agents and main customers when visiting the UK, and in their countries. Carrying very heavy bags abroad, their trips may last two, three or more weeks, and encompass half a dozen countries, thirty to forty customers or just one. They primarily sell to agents' sales managers or directors concerned with imports and may brief the agent's reps at a conference. They discuss all aspects of their trading relationship and assess agents' effectiveness. Other sales venues are the book fairs around the world.

The junior export staff, the reps, usually sell to the book trades in open markets. They try to get subscriptions for new books, do no overlook the backlist, respond to complaints and collect debts. When appropriate they supply promotion copy for inclusion in wholesalers' or retailers' catalogues, check orders in order to alleviate expensive distribution mistakes, and sometimes co-ordinate booksellers' ordering. The academic reps may additionally call on lecturers and librarians in order to secure textbook adoptions, facilitate inspection copy orders, and encourage booksellers to carry out joint promotions and exhibitions. The ELT reps promote and sell courses directly to private language schools, state schools and to government agencies.

Skills

The ability to speak preferably two or more languages is invariably needed, but is not a top priority: most customers can speak English to some extent. But linguistic ability enables you to understand and relate that much better to the market and the customers to you. Fluency in one or more of the European languages such as French, German, Spanish and Italian, and semi-fluency in some is ideal. Standard Arabic and Chinese etc. are sometimes particularly desirable for certain firms.

Export sales staff have a commitment to publishing and exporting, and have to enjoy working with books. First and foremost sales people, they have a burning desire to ring up the till, to increase profitable turnover.

Most of the personal skills required for selling to the home market are paralleled in export selling; but exporters face the complexities of understanding many different and diverse markets and need an appreciation of the political, social, economic and cultural factors pertaining to each country, as well as an empathy with, sensitivity to, and enthusiasm for the market to which they are selling or playing a part in. Good exporters are able to sell and adapt to different environments and situations fast.

In that the work involves much time abroad, exporters must like travel, have the self-motivation to work far away from headquarters, take high-level decisions on behalf of their firms, and cope with loneliness. Exporting calls for tough survivors. (Some of the overseas postings made by non-general firms are to less-developed countries with arduous climates.) With a large amount of the publisher's money in the pocket, profligacy is something employers expect you to avoid.

RIGHTS SALES

The author–publisher contract (in consumer book publishing frequently drawn up by an author's agent) delimits the scope of the publisher to license various kinds of rights to other firms. These rights allow other firms to exploit the book in different ways, media, territories and languages. The selling of rights may be done by editors and sales staff. However, medium to large publishers and packagers employ small numbers of specialists to sell rights actively.

Rights staff may also check and monitor the contracts made between the publisher and others. The reactive work involves responding to people (often authors, sometimes publishers) seeking copyright permission to reproduce material (such as extracts of text, tables, technical illustrations) from the firm's books. They are usually granted a non-exclusive licence to reproduce the material for a particular use, with due acknowledgement, for a specified quantity and in a specified language throughout the world, though the territories may be limited. The applicant is charged a fee, usually equally shared by the originating publisher and author. The advent of the Copyright Licensing Agency's Rapid Clearance Service (CLARCS) should facilitate the collection of fees from educational and other organizations wishing to photocopy extracts for class sets.

The majority of books have no significant rights sales income, but some (particularly commercial fiction and highly illustrated colour books) earn much or depend on rights deals for viability.

A small department consists of a rights manager and assistant; larger ones have staff who specialize in particular rights or regions of the world. A publisher or packager may use rights selling agents abroad (e.g. in Europe, the USA and Japan) who receive a commission of, say, 10 per cent on sales made.

Rights work involves close contact with the editorial, production, promotion and sales departments, and accounts; selling to customers (mainly editors or directors of other firms) on a regular and personal basis; processing a great deal of paperwork (e.g. correspondence, maintaining customer mailing lists, record keeping); negotiating deals and contracts; and foreign travel (at the very least attending major book fairs, Frankfurt, and – for children's books – Bologna). Staff who sell many books of international appeal (especially highly illustrated colour non-fiction) travel widely and frequently.

The rights department may get involved with a title before the author has signed the contract. An editor may ask the rights manager to assess the title's rights sales potential particularly if that affects the author's advance, or the viability of the book depends on rights sales. Around manuscript delivery titles are assessed, and a strategy drawn up regarding the choice of possible customers, how and when they will be approached. There are many kinds of rights and the deals struck are both intricate and varied. The following description of the main rights gives merely an impression. (Sometimes, the author's approval is needed before deals are concluded.)

Book club rights

Book club rights are normally granted to the publisher. A book club editor selects the books for a club's programme. They are sent sample material, often manuscripts, sometimes proofs. The publisher's aim is to secure a firm bulk order from the club early enough, so that the club's edition can be co-printed with that of its own, thereby lowering the per copy cost of production to the benefit of the margin on the trade edition. A major club will sell the book to its members at say, one-third off the publisher's catalogue price. It will reach this price by a three times mark up on the price it pays for the book (i.e. by tripling it). It therefore seeks a high discount off the publisher's catalogue price, of, say, 75–80%. The author's royalty is included in the price paid by the club, and is usually either 10% of the publisher's net receipts (which equates roughly to 2% of the publisher's catalogue price) or 50% of the manufacturing profits. Some book clubs, however, offer royalty-exclusive deals where the publisher receives a royalty of $5-7^{1}/_{2}$% based on the club price and on copies sold.

A book club may itself reprint the book under its imprint with the publisher's permission, in which case it also pays a royalty on the club price on copies sold. The royalty paid to the publishers is likewise shared with the author. In such royalty-exclusive deals the rights manager negotiates the advance payable and charges the club an offset fee (not shared with the author) for the right to reproduce the publisher's typography etc.

Book clubs invent new concepts. For example, the two quality paperback clubs take run-on sheets of the publisher's hardback edition printing and typically price their same size paperback edition for club members at 50% off the publisher's hardback catalogue price.

Regulations drawn up by The Publishers Association govern the manner of book club deals. For example, a club must order a minimum quantity of 3500 copies, or 50% of the publisher's edition (whichever is the lower) to gain an exclusive licence which is set at three years. The club is granted the exclusive right to sell its English language edition in the UK (and sometimes other overseas territories in which it operates) but is excluded from North America.

Reprint paperback rights

Owing to the emergence of consumer book publishers with their ability to publish both hardbacks and paperbacks, the selling of reprint paperback rights by originating hardback publishers to separate paperback publishers has undergone a dramatic decline. However, there is a trade in reprint rights: a small hardback publisher might sell the paperback rights to a large publisher, or an academic publisher may occasionally have a title which would attract wide-scale trade interest via a consumer book publisher.

The key features of such deals are as follows. The seller defines the rights granted, i.e. the exclusive right to publish a particular kind of edition in specified territories is stated and the duration of the licence is delimited (e.g. eight years). The buyer reprints its own edition and pays royalties on copies sold to the originating publisher. These royalties are shared between the author and the publisher, for example, 55/45 or 60/40 or 70/30 respectively. A rising royalty scale and the size of the advance (representing a proportion of future royalties) are negotiated. The advance payable is split (e.g. on signature of contract and on publication). The buyer usually pays the originating publisher an offset fee (not shared with the author) for the right to photograph the text prior to printing, and sometimes a loan fee for use of film of the illustrations. The timing of reprint paperback publication is set, so as not to undermine the originator's other sales.

US and North American rights

Authors' agents, on behalf of authors, and book packagers may retain US rights or North American rights (the USA plus Canada). But if held by the publisher and the book is not to be sold via the publisher's North American firm or through a distribution arrangement, the rights may be licensed. The USA is by far the largest and richest English language market.

Selling to US editors is carried out at a distance or personally when they visit the UK en route to Frankfurt or Bologna book fairs, or at such fairs. Sometimes, the rights manager attends the annual American Booksellers Association Convention or visits New York to see, say, five publishers per day. UK-based scouts of US publishers may be used; and UK editors are also in contact with US publishers. The submission method may be consecutive (each editor is sent the material in order) or simultaneous (the chosen editors receive the material together) or occasionally auctions are held; editors may be given a synopsis/manuscript/proofs/bound copies; and depending on the stage reached the rights manager uses the author's previous sales figures, the jacket and blurb, pre-publication quotes, the UK subscription order, reviews and other rights sales made etc. to stimulate interest.

There are essentially two types of deal. In the first the US publisher manufactures its own edition, pays royalties and an advance which are shared by the UK publisher and author – usually the larger part goes to the author. In effect the UK publisher acts as the author's agent. Additionally the US publisher may pay for the use of film of the illustrations, or an offset fee if it does not edit or Americanize the book. This type of 'royalty exclusive' deal tends to be used on most fiction and on some illustrated books of considerable US interest.

In the second, the UK publisher or packager preferably co-prints the UK edition with the US publisher's edition. The bound copies are sold at a small marked-up price; and the author's royalty of say 10% of the UK publisher's net receipts is sometimes included in the price paid. (However, a US publisher may pay royalties exclusive.) This type of deal can apply to any illustrated consumer book, and to academic books published by UK firms without a strong US presence.

Whichever applies, the US publisher is granted an exclusive licence, sometimes for the full term of copyright. The US publication date is stated, the UK publisher is obliged to supply the material by a set date, and the US publisher, too, to publish by a certain date. Attempts are made to forestall premature release of an ensuing US paperback or remainder, which could jeopardize export sales of a UK paperback. The price paid or the royalty rates, and advance, are negotiated as well as the territories. The US publisher is granted exclusively the USA (with Canada open to negotiation), is excluded from the UK publisher's territories (e.g. the Commonwealth and mainland Europe), and has the non-exclusive right to publish in other countries. The US publisher may be granted other rights (e.g. book club, reprint paperback, serial) and pays a proportionate sum from such sales to the UK publisher (then shared with the author like the royalties). With some co-edition deals the US publisher may be territorially limited to North America, and the subsidiary rights granted too may be fewer.

Translation rights

In the case of adult consumer books, these rights (for some or all foreign languages) are often retained by agents and by book packagers. North European language editions may increase export sales of the English language edition owing to the book's increased exposure. Dutch language editions, on the other hand, may have the opposite effect. But if they are held by the publisher, the titles are promoted abroad by catalogue rights guide, letter, fax and telephone, and personally at major book fairs. Publishers within a language market area are selected, given priority, ranked and sent material consecutively – each may be given an option (the exclusive sight of the book for a period, say one to three months, to make a decision). Academic/STM titles take some time to be reviewed. For highly saleable books, material may be sent to publishers simultaneously.

In many cases the foreign publisher translates and produces the book (and may be charged for the film of the illustrations), pays royalties and an advance (usually lower than English rights), or occasionally a lump sum to reproduce a set quantity; is granted an exclusive language licence for a particular edition, and other rights, for a set period throughout the world. Sometimes, on a consumer book, a Spanish or French publisher is excluded from Latin America or Québec, respectively.

The alternative deal used for many highly illustrated colour books and children's picture books, is for the foreign language publishers to supply typeset film of their translations to fit around the four-colour illustrations. Several language editions are preferably co-printed together by the publisher or packager in order to gain economies of scale. The printing press usually has five cylinders carrying the printing plates. Four cylinders carry the plates which print the four-colour illustrations (made up of yellow, magenta, cyan and black), and the fifth cylinder carries the plate of the text printed in black outside the areas of the illustrations. The press operator changes the fifth plate for each language edition printing. The ordered quantities, carrying each publisher's imprint, are often supplied royalty inclusive, possibly exclusive.

The co-edition deals made with English and foreign language publishers are central to the work of rights staff of highly illustrated adult and children's publishers and packagers. They usually initiate deals well in advance of publication with English language publishers and book clubs first, using the future book's contents, and mock-ups of the jacket and selected double-page spreads etc. The co-printing of foreign language editions follows because these publishers translate from the English ozalid proof or the bound copy. The English and foreign language co-printing of children's books of few words can coincide. Negotiations with customers on the price paid per copy for the books, the timing of the deals and their combined printing are critical. The complexity of these deals, involving close contact with the UK publisher's or packager's own production/design departments, and those overseas, makes it difficult for authors' agents to enter this form of rights selling.

Serial and extract rights

First serial rights (the most valuable because they appear before the book's publication and offer a national newspaper or magazine a scoop) are often but not always retained by authors' agents, sometimes by packagers. The second and subsequent serial rights (usually granted to a publisher) appear after book publication and may be sold to a succession of regional or evening newspapers, or magazines, at rates equal to or above that paid for original articles of comparable length. Ideas for extracts, which may come from the editor, are marked on the manuscript or proof and are sent to chosen journalists, with first serial rights twelve to six months ahead of book publication. The author's share of first serial rights (often as much as 90%) may be offset against the advance, so as well as providing valuable publicity for the book the sale of such serial rights is particularly valuable financially.

Other rights

Examples include film, television, radio, video and audiocassette rights; merchandising rights (e.g. characters from the book appearing on other kinds of product); large print rights; promotional reprint rights and English language paperback licensing rights to export territories.

The licensing of electronic media rights is in its infancy. Publishers are beginning to receive permission requests from, for example, multimedia producers and the universities to reproduce material in various electronic media.

Some publishers may sub-license whole works, preferably not the family silver, and try to protect themselves by granting short term, non-exclusive or narrow exclusive licences, in particular languages, limited to specific formats or platforms, with performance guarantees and advances. Alternatively they may enter into joint ventures in which costs and income are shared in agreed proportions.

Skills

Rights staff preferably know French and/or German, and if concerned with co-editions especially, Italian and Spanish as well. But negotiations are in English (except with the French). However senior, the work involves typing and much administration.

The essential prerequisite of selling is knowing the books and the customers. Editorial insight of the firm's new titles and lateral thinking aids the assessment of rights prospects and their worth, the drawing out of salient points and the realization of sales revenue. With highly saleable titles, skilled judgement is needed on the kind of approach and its timing to selected customers.

The perception of customers' needs entails an understanding of the way they run different kinds of businesses (e.g. product range, markets and financial structure) in different cultural, political and economic contexts; and of their personal interests.

Dealing with relatively small numbers of senior people regularly and personally demands the development of good and close relations. Sales skills encompass the enthusiastic promotion of titles in writing, on the telephone and in person, even when there is scant information available on a new title. Where customers are in competition or when time is short in co-printing, they have to be pressured and manoeuvred to clinch deals quickly.

Negotiation skills allied to experience, numeracy and fast thinking help a rights person to tell if a customer is offering too low an advance or too little in a co-printing deal. The full implications and catches in customer contracts must be spotted and adverse clauses removed or modified.

Where physical elements are supplied, the knowledge of production processes and of terminology are required. As so much of the job involves remembering and recording which books are on offer and who is looking at what, a meticulous, methodical mind which registers fine detail is essential – the consequences of selling the same book twice in the same territory are horrendous.

Long working days precede and follow the major fairs, such as Frankfurt, at which customers are seen on half-hourly appointments during the day, and informally into the nights, over a week. The job calls for immense stamina and a strong voice box.

DISTRIBUTION, ACCOUNTS, PERSONNEL AND COMPUTER STAFF

Distribution

The distribution of the books, journals and other new technology products is inherent to the publisher's role of getting its products into the customers' hands at the right time and in the right quantities. The key aspects of distribution are customer care, accuracy in order fulfilment, speed and reliability in despatch, the physical protection of the product and economies in despatch. Failings in these areas lead to lost sales, diminished retail display, increased cost to the publisher and loss of confidence by bookseller and reader; improvements give the publisher a competitive marketing edge.

Book publishers' distribution is an enormous challenge and exhibits most unusual characteristics. Many other kinds of goods produced by manufacturers (often on continuous production lines) are supplied via wholesalers to retailers, whereas publishers for their size carry an enormous range of new and backlist products and store it for a long time. In the main publishers supply retailers directly. Wholesaling is relatively weak in the UK and is concentrated on consumer books. Publishers' customers extend beyond the book trade – to schools and to individuals needing single copies (e.g. review, inspection, mail-order sales). Publishers receive massive numbers of small orders, the profits from which does not cover the distribution and credit cost. Yet book retailers demand faster and more reliable distribution in order to compete against other kinds of products. UK publishers export vigorously and distribute to most countries from the UK via a myriad of arrangements and carriers. In material handling terms, book distribution presents extremes, ranging from one or more titles of varying size or other media products up to a container load. Publishers, especially of consumer books, face the return of unsold books from the book trade, which are credited accordingly; and if the books are damaged or of low value they destroy them.

Traditionally, publishers' distribution has been slow, erratic and inaccurate; its cost became an increasing burden. Booksellers waited many weeks for the arrival of orders, and during the run-up to Christmas reps often delivered stock by car. Hundreds of publishers operated their own distribution, delivering direct to booksellers. The distribution chain, engaging a mass of paper-work, was like a cat's cradle. However, in the 1980s, the process speeded up so that today some publishers manage a seven-day turn-around for orders, and at critical times of year accelerated services are offered by tertiary textbook publishers in the autumn and by consumer book publishers before Christmas. Greater efficiencies have resulted from the merging of publishers as well as from the emergence of independent distributors serving smaller publishers, pace-selling wholesalers in the consumer book field and highly competitive and quick national carriers (now extending into Europe); and the application of electronics.

The foundation stone on which all book trade electronic transactions and information systems are based was the introduction in 1967 of the Standard Book Number (SBN). By 1970 it had become internationally accepted. The ISBN incorporates the language of origin, the publisher, and the unique identifier of each book or edition (the last digit is a check to ensure the preceding digits are correct). In 1979, Teleordering was launched. This enabled booksellers to transmit orders electronically overnight into publishers' computers. Teleordering was the book trade's first proprietary electronic trading system deploying an early form of Electronic Data Interchange. EDI facilitates the exchange of data between computer systems, saving trading partners time, errors and cost by avoiding the use and handling of paper and making it unnecessary to re-key information.

By the mid-1980s standards were developed to convert the ISBN into the European Article Numbering (EAN) bar code. This appears on the back cover of books. By the early 1990s most main UK bookshops had installed electronic point of sale (EPoS) systems which read the bar codes. Booksellers thus have an electronic means to tell them which books are selling and how quickly, which books are not selling, and potentially how much margin they are making per foot of shelf space in relation to different publishers' discounts and price levels.

In the drive towards electronic ordering, invoicing, information gathering and transmission, Book Industry Communication (BIC) was founded by The Publishers Association, The Booksellers Association, The Library Association and British Library.

The aims of BIC include the development and promotion of standard EDI formats. Its first tasks are to facilitate electronic trading (e.g. orders, acknowledgements, delivery notes, invoices, credit notes, and price and availability updates) between booksellers and publishers, booksellers and wholesalers, and libraries and their suppliers, in the UK and later across Europe and other developed markets; and secondly to draw up standards for the content of publishers' bibliographic databases and for the transmission of product information to bibliographers and libraries to facilitate marketing.

New generation bar codes, able to hold several thousand characters of information, offer the prospect of encoding a complex delivery note on a carton of books, or bibliographic information on a book itself; or the contents of a journal which could, for instance, be fed directly into a library database. Machine readable bar codes are at the heart of EDI, be it in the publisher's warehouse or at the point of sale.

The use of electronic trading and standard EDI formats offer a publisher feedback on the buying habits and interests of customers useful to its marketing/sales departments. However, while publishers know what they are selling into bookshops, they have little idea whether or not stock is selling out of them. On the one hand, consumer book publishers face returns of overstocked books, and on the other are sometimes caught out-of-stock at crucial times by books that sell surprisingly fast. They cannot reprint quickly enough to meet demand. The nationwide collection of sales data from booksellers' EPoS systems, broken down by geographic area and subject category, will make publishers and booksellers immediately aware of the sales pattern of individual titles, and of market trends.

BIC is also examining the data held in library management systems in order to assess the value of that data in assisting libraries, publishers and library suppliers. EDI may be used by the Copyright Licensing Agency in the handling of permission clearances; and BIC is working with universities and libraries in the use of cable networks to link academic and journal publishers in the supply of information to the academic community, and of electronic document delivery in due course.

While EDI initiatives will be vital aids in distributing and selling books, universal electronic trading and invoicing is some way off, and publishers and booksellers have yet to manage together the supply and **return** chain of books so costly to all parties. However, booksellers' EPoS systems since the early 1990s have prompted them to want just-in-time deliveries. They order smaller quantities more frequently. On the one hand, the smaller the value of the order and the faster the service, the greater is the distribution cost. On the other, publishers unable to fulfil that service lose out. All of these trends are leading to fewer and larger distributors. Size gives to the distributor the turnover to invest in expensive electronic, book handling and warehouse systems, the ability to bulk up order values, greater leverage in debt collection, and the securing of lower rates with carriers. With the development of faster and more reliable transportation systems, including air freight, there is a movement away from overseas stockholding agents to direct supply from the UK, giving a greater opportunity to price books more competitively in many markets.

The major publishing groups run their own distribution and generally place the facility in the country away from head-quarters. Medium and small publishers may also carry out their own distribution. They, however, increasingly use independent distributors, or larger publishers, or wholesalers – all of which are eager to increase their turnover. While such firms usually offer a complete service, some smaller publishers may carry out the order-processing and invoicing themselves, using the distributor for bulk storage and despatch.

The 'trade side' of distribution is concerned with processing received orders, raising invoices and documentation. Not all publishers can accept teleorders, and many orders are received in writing or by fax, telephone etc. Thus there are order editors who clarify ambiguities in orders. The orders are loaded on to computer, so that the invoice, documentation, labelling and physical distribution begin. There are many standardized codes which tell a customer a book is unavailable for various reasons. UK booksellers are identified by the Standard Address Number (SAN) which is a unique identifier of the delivery address. New books or reprints not yet in stock are recorded on a 'dues listing' and despatched when available unless otherwise instructed. Export orders need additional documentation to comply with the receiving country's import regulations and taxes, such as VAT. On orders to mainland Europe some main publishers invoice in local currencies and offer banking arrangements. Mistakes in export orders incur severe penalties. (Pro-forma invoices may be sent to unsafe customers before the books are dispatched.) Most publishers supply books to UK booksellers carriage free.

The customer services department resolves queries from sometimes irate booksellers regarding problems of distribution and of accounts. The textbook inspection copy service and mail-order or subscription sales are usually handled by separate departments.

The warehouse includes the bulk store of books (and of any raw paper reserves) into which suppliers' deliveries are made and a 'picking' area where titles and back-up stock are positioned for easy location (new books and fast-selling titles in prime sites). The invoices may include the location of titles in the order in which they are 'picked' (gathered ready for despatch). The collated orders move to the packaging and despatch area. Despatch involves knowing the most economic, quickest and reliable method (e.g. road carrier, shipping, air freight, post and negotiating bulk deals with carriers). If the publisher bears the cost, the incentive is to lower costs to increase profitability; when the customers pays (e.g. on FOB export orders) the incentive is to assist them save money, a marketing service. In order to treat mainland Europe as an extension of the home market and to compete against US publishers, some UK publishers are using pan-European delivery networks being set up by the same carriers as used in the UK. In so doing, the publisher controls the level of service door-to-door, avoids dealing with dozens of carriers (which can be appointed by retailers) and attains economies.

While the computer monitors stock levels, there are staff who physically check the stock and check the returns (the bar codes can aid the task), liaising with the sales office where appropriate.

The application of computers to order-processing, distribution and despatch provides key information for management, such as reports on dues, sales by title, area, by representative (and comparative monthly reports), type of customer, discount structure, return levels, stock and re-order levels, method of despatch, carriage charge analysis, debtors etc.

Finance and accounts

All firms of any size need accounts staff to handle the payroll, tax, pension scheme etc. and to deal with the firm's financial activities with its suppliers (e.g. printers, freelancers and authors) and customers. The credit control staff assess and set new customers' credit limits, monitor their performance, debt chase and liaise closely with the sales department especially when UK and overseas customers are placed on the stop list. A bookseller placed on a stop list and denied any further deliveries is most likely to tell a customer that the book requested by the customer is out-of-print rather than admit to debts. The quick recovery of debts is a vital factor in aiding the firm's cashflow and improving its profitability. The costing section of an accounts department is concerned with monitoring book costings at the publishing proposal stage, subsequently comparing actual costs against estimates, and preparing book profit and loss statements.

The royalty section is particular to publishing (and larger literary agencies) and the staff have a rarity value. They have copies of the author–publisher contracts, and the contracts covering rights sales (the buyers are pressed for settlement so that the income can be apportioned). Different royalties due to the author from the publisher's edition are calculated by applying the contractual details to the title's sales record. Sums owed by the author (e.g. for excessive proof corrections, or for books purchased) are deducted from royalties and the royalty statement prepared. If authors have the royalty paid in advance, it is similarly set against the royalty income. On some titles, the income from sales never reaches or surpasses the advance paid, in which case the unearned sum owed by the author to the publisher is written off. While some publishers, especially in the consumer book field, hold a reserve of royalties to set against future returns of books from retailers, an author may be paid royalties on copies which are later returned. Such sums owing are carried over to the following royalty statement, but at the end of the book's life are usually written off. A royalty manager, conversant with current double taxation relief, overseas tax regulations and VAT and able to explain their ramifications, patiently, tactfully, clearly and promptly inspires authors and agents with confidence, and is invaluable to the publisher.

The finance director and senior accountants are responsible for producing the annual statutory accounts, and for strategic financial management. They monitor the cashflow, analyse and interpret the firm's financial performance (assisted by many indices) against budgets and past figures, for top-level management decisions which affect the evaluation of new projects. The large groups usually centralize this service, and their senior staff examine take-over targets.

Personnel

Personnel departments which deal with staff recruitment policy, discipline, development and training (including the introduction of National Vocational Qualifications) tend to be restricted to large publishers. In smaller firms these tasks form part of the work of an office manager, or of the managing director's office etc.

Computers

Computers were first used in the order-processing and accounts and royalty departments, and specialists were engaged in data-processing. Later, other departments gained on-line access to the data (e.g. sales and stock levels). Increasingly, however, networked or free-standing computers are used in the preparation of catalogues and sales letters etc., production office costing and scheduling, reference book databases (for exploitation in print and electronic form), and in the editorial and design areas. Although software is usually bought in, publishers may need their own in-house experts to facilitate or modify its use.

The business of publishing

From a financial viewpoint, the senior management strives to increase the rate at which capital is earned and turned over and to improve the profit margin for expansion and for the owners; for example, its members try to:

- maximize the income and minimize the production costs;
- contain royalty rates while keeping competitive, in consumer book publishing monitor the amount of money and level of risk tied up in authors' advances in relation to actual sales;
- control prudently the stock levels (just sufficient to service sales) by selling a high proportion of a print number on publication or soon after, and storing only adequate stock of backlist titles that sell;
- re-price regularly the backlist titles (usually upwards) in line with current prices;
- control tightly the firm's overheads (e.g. staff and office costs) while maintaining effective management: if profits fall, overheads have to be reduced and output increased;
- take all available credit from suppliers (e.g. authors and printers);
- keep discounts as low as possible (while customers will demand increases) and costs of returns but, at the same time, maintain display space in customers' outlets;
- collect debts quickly from customers;
- obtain the best terms from capital providers (e.g. banks);
- invest in fixed assets (e.g. warehouses, computers) only if a favourable return can be shown in comparison with sub-contracting or leasing;
- sell off under-used or under-performing assets (e.g. buildings, lists/imprints);

- buy complementary businesses at home and abroad;
- forecast regularly the cashflow (the flow of money payments to, from, or within the firm) over time; even a profitable publisher can exceed its borrowing requirement before profits are earned and go bust.

One key aspect is the compilation, say at least six months ahead, of a financial plan showing a profit target for the forthcoming year (or longer). It is built up partly from the historic costs of running the business and from forecasts (e.g. the estimated costs of producing the new titles – authors' advances, royalties and production costs, and their timing; and the revenue from estimated sales made through various channels at home and abroad, over time; similarly for backlist titles – their costs and sales revenue over time). Furthermore the departmental managers prepare budgets for carrying out their activities.

Actual performance is compared regularly with the plan at, say, monthly intervals, and with the performance of the previous year's; and the plan itself is updated. Some long-term publishers (e.g. textbook or reference) compile rolling plans for up to five years ahead.

PROFIT AND LOSS STATEMENT: PUBLISHER'S COST PROFILE

The annual profit and loss statement of a publisher reveals the cost profile of the business as a whole, and each publisher's differs. Furthermore such statements of different kinds of publisher (adult general, childrens, educational, academic etc.) differ in aggregate, reflecting the different nature of their businesses – the following figures give an impression.

The total net sales revenue (NSR) is the sum of money the publisher receives from home and export sales after the discounts have been deducted from the published prices. Taking the NSR as 100% and subtracting from that the production costs of the books (say around 30%, plus or minus 5%) plus the write-off of stock unsold (say 2–10%) and the cost of royalties (10–15%), leaves the publisher with a gross profit of say 45–55%. (While a consumer book publisher may suffer from the write-off of unrecoverable authors' advances, it may benefit from significant rights sales income.) From the gross trading profit, the publisher's costs are deducted: e.g. editorial 8–10%; production and design 2–3%; publicity and sales staff 6%; promotion expenditure 5%; sales commission 1–3%; order processing and distribution 10–13%; general and administrative expenses 4–7%. These overheads and expenses roughly total 39–47% which when deducted from the gross trading profit leaves the publisher with a net profit (before interest charges on borrowing and tax are deducted) of say 9–12%. After interest and tax, a dividend may be paid to shareholders and the remaining profit re-invested in the business. During recessions net profitability declines and even during buoyant periods some publishers make a loss, while others reap net profits much higher than that above.

The publisher's overheads and expenses are very important, not just because they must be tightly controlled from one year to another (monitored in response to changing work practices and salary increases etc.) and kept in line with those of competing publishers in the field, but because they should be apportioned to and recovered from each new book – at least in theory. Successful publishing is founded on contracting good books that sell and each new book is a business in its own right. The decision to take on a new book, its costing and pricing prior to contract were touched on in Chapter 4. The decision to publish is the crux of the whole enterprise. If bad mistakes are made here, all efforts of management to control overheads will come to nothing. The sum total of profits of all the new book proposals must equal, preferably exceed, the publisher's overall profit target. Thus new books which are planned at the outset, but fail in reality, to achieve the target must be counterbalanced by equal profits from other books which exceed their target.

Two general ways of pricing books are the gross profit and the unit cost mark-up methods.

COSTING A BOOK: GROSS PROFIT (OR GROSS MARGIN) METHOD

In essence, this method mirrors the profit and loss statement. Put crudely, the management may say to their editors, 'We want to see each publishing proposal attaining a gross profit of (e.g. 55–60+%)'. That percentage represents the sum of money the publisher would have left after the production costs and author's royalties have been deducted from the NSR, provided all the copies were sold. That money would then, in theory, be sufficient to recover the overheads and expenses (expressed in overall percentages) and to provide a net profit as follows.

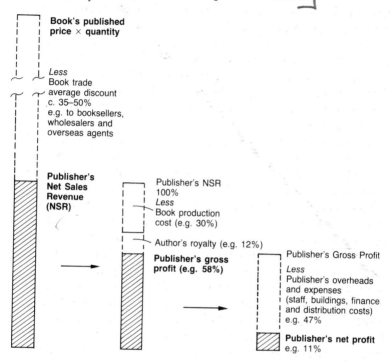

Who gets what in the book business

Note: The publisher's *Net Sales Revenue* (NSR) is the sum of money the publisher receives after the trade discounts have been deducted, and its *gross profit* is what is left after the costs of production and royalty have been deducted. The publisher's *net profit* should be the sum finally left after all the costs of running the business have been deducted.

At the outset of the calculation the editor considers the book's desired physical attributes, the costs of production, and the possible prices and sales potential in unison. Here they are separated.

The income

Factors affecting the book's possible published price include its perceived value to end-users; their ability to pay low or high prices (e.g. high earning professionals); competitors' books (especially if the book can be compared against similar books in shops, rather than stand alone by mail order); its uniqueness; whether the book will be bought primarily by end-users or by libraries or businesses; and whether there are established price ceilings in the market which, if breached, could reduce sales (e.g. to an impulse buyer, gift buyer, student or school etc.).

The raising of a published price would usually lead to a fall in the quantity demanded, whereas lowering the price would usually (but not always) lead to a rise in the quantity demanded. Books which are thought to be 'price inelastic' (i.e. changing the price has only a limited effect on the level of demand) tend to be highly specialist and professional titles while many consumer books, especially paperbacks, bought on impulse, and many textbooks, tend to be 'price elastic' (i.e. changing the price has a greater effect on the level of demand). The price elasticities of various kinds of book differ. (It can be difficult for an editor to persuade an academic or professional book author that lowering the price would not open the gates to a flood of eager readers.)

If a book were greatly overpriced, few copies would be sold and a low revenue results; if the price fell within a market price band, changing the price would have a greater effect on demand; but if the price were fixed even lower, the level of demand fails to respond as the market for the book reaches saturation, the total revenue falls again. Thus if one objective is to maximize the firm's income, a published price and a sales forecast which when multiplied together produce the maximum revenue, are aimed for.

The sales forecast is related to a time period. Publishers print stock sufficient for a limited period only (say six to eighteen months, or for mass market paperbacks under three months).

The net sales revenue is calculated by multiplying the sales forecasts for the home market and the export market by the published price less the discounts. While each book is sold at many discounts, an average discount derived from all the trans-actions by the firm is applied (e.g. for a consumer book 43% on home sales, 50% plus on export sales). The average on some books (e.g. those sold particularly to high discount customers) would be adjusted upwards. The revenue from any co-edition deals made at very high discounts to other firms (e.g. UK book clubs or US publishers) which order in advance bulk quantities of bound copies from the publisher, are included, as would be the inter-company sales to overseas firms that are part of an international group, such as in the academic/STM fields.

The costs

The costs of producing a book usually come under two headings. The 'fixed costs' are incurred before the printing presses roll and do not change whatever the quantity of books ordered. They may include: sums paid to external readers; translators; permission fees for the use of third-party copyright material (text and illustrations); payments to freelances (e.g. editors, illustrators, designers); and major payments to print suppliers for typesetting, origination of illustrations, proofing, corrections, imposition, plates etc.

The 'variable costs' occur after the presses start to roll and depend on the quantity of books ordered. They include the costs of printing and binding, and the paper consumed. The quantity ordered would be the sales estimate plus an allowance for copies wasted or given away for review etc.

Roughly speaking, the fixed costs account for a third to a half of the total production costs on consumer books and textbooks, and more than half on short-run professional titles and scientific research.

The cost of producing each copy, 'the unit cost' (the print quantity divided into the total cost), diminishes with increasing print quantities. The unit cost falls rapidly on short printings of between, say, 700 to 2500 copies and then more slowly. The rapid decline in unit cost results not from the variable cost but from the fixed costs being spread over larger quantities. Although the per copy cost of producing the book becomes progressively lower with increasing quantities, the total cost increases in a near linear relationship.

The costs of author's royalties are calculated by applying the different royalty rates to the sales forecasts for home and export markets etc.

Combining the income and costs

The editor strives to balance the income and costs so that the desired gross profit is attained. If too low, the production costs could be reduced (e.g. shorter book, fewer illustrations, cheaper paper etc.) or the author's proposed royalties cut. Conversely, the price and sales estimate could be increased. But while the publisher worries about costs and margins, the end-user is concerned with price and perceived value, and does not care about the costs, the number printed or the author's effort. For an editor publishing a book with a limited market, there is the fatal temptation to imagine a non-existent larger market and to increase the print-run in order to lower unit cost.

The book's peak profitability may occur at a slightly lower sales figure than the number which yields the maximum revenue, owing to the increased costs of producing that quantity. The publisher could choose a lower published price which increased sales but the revenue from that may not recover the increased costs. The publisher could have made a profit if only it had not printed too many copies in excess of actual demand.

When the publisher takes the final decision on fixing the price and print quantity (and it has only one chance of getting it right), the fixed costs have already been incurred and cannot be changed.

On account of the uncertainties of estimating demand a prudent publisher favours a higher price and a lower quantity rather than a lower price and a higher quantity. If the actual demand for the book is less than expected, a price on the high side may still return a profit, whereas too low a price could lead to substantial loss. The great dangers are underestimating costs, overestimating demand and printing too many copies, and underpricing. This leads not only to a loss on the individual book, but can wipe out the profit on others. Successful books can always be reprinted, but at a price and quantity which again are chosen to avoid loss.

Other factors entering the pre-publication decisions concern the amount of investment at risk (e.g. very high authors' advances, or a large investment in a major reference book or textbook), and its duration. The calculation of 'worst case scenarios' or of the project's break-even point (e.g. the minimum quantity that must be sold to cover the production costs, author's advance or royalty, plus a proportion of overhead) can show the level of risk. On some proposals, if break-even is considered attainable, that may inspire sufficient confidence to go ahead. Some publishers calculate a project's cashflow and the interest incurred over time. From the outset to after publication, the publisher usually endures a net loss before the income surpasses the outlay. The estimated income is derived from the sales forecasts broken down over time (e.g. monthly, quarterly, yearly).

Possible rights sales income, other than that from co-printing deals, usually does not enter into the early costings and thus can be regarded as extra profit. However, it may be included, especially when needed to justify paying the author a large advance.

The costing exercise may apply to more than one edition (e.g. hardback and paperback editions on which most of the fixed costs have been carried on the back of the hardback edition) or to more than one printing (e.g. the first printing of a school textbook may attain no profit, but the hoped-for second and subsequent printings should move into profitability).

Some publishers stop their calculations at the gross profit line while others continue and deduct direct overheads expressed as overall percentages (e.g. editorial/design/production; and promotion and sales) to reach the net profit. The way in which overheads are apportioned, either as actual sums or percentages, varies.

The problems with the gross profit method as outlined above are that titles are allocated overheads in proportion to expected revenue (which may not accord with reality); it focuses attention on a desired percentage rather than money (e.g. a title may attain only a 25% gross profit yet deliver much more cash than one with a 55% gross profit); it encourages a minimum objective (there is nothing wrong in achieving a 100% profit); and it assumes a steady state.

COSTING A BOOK: UNIT COST MARK-UP METHOD

This traditional and simple method is severely criticized but can be used as a ready-reckoner. Essentially, the unit, or per copy, print production cost (derived from dividing the quantity of books to be ordered into the total cost of printing those books, i.e. the fixed production costs plus the variable cost of that quantity) is multiplied by a factor (e.g. 5, 6, 8) to arrive at the published price. The accounts department calculate for editors the factors pertaining to different kinds of books (e.g. consumer or academic) with different royalty rates and discounts. Provided the copies sell out the factor accommodates the firm's costs and profit. But if the published price is thought too high, the editor is tempted to increase the print run to lower unit cost in order to arrive, by multiplication, at a reasonable price. Conversely, the publishers may print the number it believes it can sell but fix the price too high to absorb that number. Unless careful the publisher ends up with unsold copies or loss-makers. The method, based on a predetermined level of activity, disregards the fact that costs do not act alike as output increases or decreases, encourages rigid pricing and conceals assumptions. Worse, it focuses attention on unit cost and away from the market and price elasticities.

The method can be used in reverse. The gross retail value (price multiplied by sales estimate) is divided by the factor to arrive at the desired unit cost. The book's specification could then be adjusted to match.

The use of a mark-up factor often occurs when consumer book publishers buy books from packagers (e.g. a mark-up factor of between 4 and 5 is applied to the packager's all in, royalty-inclusive, price per copy to arrive at a published price; or if the publisher is translating and resetting, five or six). The packager seeks the lowest mark-up factor attainable.

SUCCESSES, NON-CONTRIBUTORS AND FAILURES

If a book is reprinted and the publisher has recovered all its development costs and fixed costs from the first printing, its margin (provided the copies sell out) dramatically increases (because such costs do not recur). But substantially revised new editions incur renewed fixed costs and relaunch overheads. Publishing is a high margin business and can be immensely profitable. But for numerous publishers, those profits are a mirage – they make just too many mistakes.

Some authors either fail to deliver manuscripts or submit unacceptable material. The consumer book publishers which pay significant sums on signature of contract, can find them difficult to recover; in some rare cases they are victims of fraudulent authors. If a proposed book is not published, its estimated contribution to overheads needs to be recouped from elsewhere. It is relatively easier for a consumer book publisher to fill its list more quickly (e.g. by buying from packagers or from US firms) than a school textbook publisher. All the decisions regarding the quality of a book, its market, price and sales potential are based on advance subjective judgements. Among the new books there inevitably lurk those that fail to recover their production costs or the author's advance, let alone make a contribution to overheads. Generally speaking, publishers make very little net profit from their new book publishing programme over the first year. Their profits stem from the surviving titles that reprint.

A vigorous and profitable publisher is in a strong position to publish books which, it is estimated at the outset, will not show a profit; indeed there may be good publishing reasons for doing so. A book could be published for prestige purposes. A fiction publisher may believe in a novelist's long-term ultimate success, of want the author's next more desirable book. A textbook publisher may want to enter a new area and undercut competitors. A university press may be obliged to publish a great scholarly work (sometimes supported by a subvention). Some publishers keep titles in print even though the storage costs exceed their revenue. For example a fiction publisher may keep in print an author's body of work, and a university press may keep scholarly titles in print for years.

6

Getting into publishing and career pathways

YOUR CAREER CAMPAIGN

Although so many junior jobs advertised state that previous publishing experience is necessary, entry to publishing is paradoxically mainly at the bottom. You should therefore snatch any kind of work in any area of publishing, whatever the size of firm. Publishers usually recruit only to fill vacancies which, at the entry level, often occur at no more than a month's notice. Once in, you will be learning, gaining personal impressions of various jobs by talking to people, and, what is more, be in a position to hear about future jobs. From that bridgehead, it is usually easier to obtain a second job than the first, by moving sideways or upwards within or outside the firm. Do not fear that your first job, or jobs, will necessarily determine your subsequent career. Two to three job changes in the first five years are not uncommon. But at the outset, it is preferable to think firstly of the kinds of books you would be interested in publishing and hence the type of publishing company, and secondly the kind of work for which you feel you might have a particular aptitude.

To increase your chances, the ability to drive is useful and typing/wordprocessing and computer literacy is necessary for the great number of junior jobs.

During vacations, try proofreading for an academic etc., offer your services to short-staffed booksellers. (If you are a bookseller and want to cross to publishing, two to three years of bookselling is ample.) A temporary job with a publisher during the summer may lead to the elusive first full-time appointment.

Market research

You must carry out research on publishing in general and on an individual publisher or a group of target publishers in particular, and especially you should research the books these firms publish.

Read the trade press; examine the most recent trade directories; read book reviews; and visit libraries and bookshops to look at the books on the shelves and to seek advice on books from librarians and booksellers. For specialist areas visit the appropriate library or bookshop. When visiting bookshops during quiet periods try to talk to the book buyer who deals directly with publishers' reps.

The most useful compendium of publishers' books is the twice yearly special issues of *The Bookseller: Spring Books Issue,* and *Autumn Books Issue.* These bumper issues may be available behind the counter of a library or bookshop. Notable absences are the book packagers and the educational publishers. To trace the latter you could attend one of the annual subject-related or regional conferences at which publishers exhibit. The annual spring London Book Fair provides a great opportunity to view the wares of publishers and packagers, and the venue to meet their staff – arrive early.

When you have narrowed down the field or have secured an interview, you must read the publisher's catalogue before any further approach is made.

If possible visit the publisher's showroom to examine the books and collect catalogues. While a kind bookseller or possibly a librarian of a large library may show you catalogues, a better course of action would be to obtain the appropriate catalogues from a publisher's publicity department or from the person who has placed the advertisement.

Making contacts

Contacts in publishing (and to a less extent with authors, literary agents, printers, booksellers, review and trade press journalists) can provide insight into particular firms, offering you advice, spreading knowledge of your abilities, and alerting you to impending vacancies. Sometimes these contacts are influential enough to secure you a preliminary discussion or interview, though rarely a job itself. Therefore, first tap your family and personal connections; if you draw a blank there, take the initiative. You can make contacts and learn by joining the London-based Society of Young Publishers (SYP). It holds monthly meetings – at which senior publishers pronounce – and publishes the journal, *Inprint*. Membership is not restricted to people employed in publishing. Women in Publishing (WiP) holds regular meetings and training sessions in London and Oxford. Membership is open to women of any age in publishing. You may be able to attend meetings of the Independent Publishers Guild (IPG) in London and around the country (mainly small publishers and packagers), the Society of Picture Researchers and Editors (SPREd), the Galley Club, the Publishers Publicity Circle, the Rights Circle, the Children's Book Circle, the Business Publishers Group and the South Coast Publishers Group (see *Directories* and *The Bookseller* for addresses). Most of the publishing luncheon and dining clubs are private. However, The Paternosters has no barriers to entry and its members meet for lunch monthly in London to enjoy their company and to listen to distinguished speakers (contact David Hale, The Coach House, Cleves Lane, Upton Grey, Hants RG25 2RG, telephone 0256 862833).

The relevance of a degree

The number of people in publishing with degrees has increased markedly. The last area in which change has been slower is in home sales of consumer book publishers. Most new editors have degrees and in academic editing a degree may be thought to be most relevant but even in those areas a degree is not essential for successful publishing. But many publishers faced with so many hopefuls use a degree qualification as a simple device for sorting out applicants. Those without degrees can still enter, for instance via the secretarial or sales routes, or with relevant work experience (such as in print production).

People with degrees in science, mathematics and other specialities, such as law or medicine, are at a premium for publishers in those areas. A teaching background and/or experience in English language teaching is particularly useful for educational/ ELT publishers, and African studies (or Voluntary Service Overseas) for international educational publishers. Qualification in cartography is useful for map and guide publishers. Language degrees are desirable for rights and export sales departments of all kinds of publishers.

The level of degree is less important. Those with doctorates seeking their first junior job may face the difficulty that they are that much older than competing applicants, though some get in.

Very few large publishers recruit graduate trainees. They generally aim to offer them accelerated diverse experience but generally a job is not guaranteed after training.

Pre-entry training

Traditionally, the only departments in which formal vocationally orientated qualifications are very desirable are graphic design and production. Many publishers believe new entrants can learn other publishing skills on the job from their colleagues and seniors. The pre-entry publishing courses used to be restricted mainly to a small number of printing, art and design and technical colleges and polytechnics, and usually concentrated on copy-editing and production skills. However, by the end of the 1980s the established institutions broadened their course content to include the business and marketing aspects of publishing; and they incorporated greater academic rigour, sometimes enabling students to study publishing along with other disciplines. The expansion of higher education in the early 1990s and the establishment of the 'new universities' has increased the number and range of courses available at undergraduate, post-graduate and diploma levels (see Appendix), with student places around several hundred per year. The full degree courses tend to be the most comprehensive academically and incorporate practical editing skills (including DTP etc.), while the shorter diploma courses presented by former technical colleges tend to be more practically orientated. The institutions recognize the importance of personal skills in information technology (IT); publishing studies can be combined with broader business studies and the effects of IT, and languages; or can be a minor part of media/information studies.

Attaining a qualification does not guarantee a job in book publishing but it substantially increases the chances – the established institutions scored impressive success rates even during the recession of the early 1990s. A high proportion of publishing graduates enter financial service industries (e.g. banks and building societies), advertising agencies and magazine publishers, the starting salaries of which are higher than in book publishing.

Secretarial entry

Secretarial jobs are spread evenly across departments. The number of secretarial posts is declining due to the advent of PCs and E-mail, and the ability of managers and editors to use their own wordprocessing and spread sheet programs, and the pressures to cut staff costs. When publishers recruit secretaries they are doing just that and are not making any promises about promotion. Publishers want their secretaries to have a good level of education and literacy, with accurate spelling and punctuation. Most want A level qualifications, such as English, and some favour degrees. The employment of the newly graduated with competent skills is a particular feature in London and Oxford. However, some London-based publishers still prefer to take people who start with them after A levels and build up to senior level rather than graduate secretaries who may be over-qualified and pushing for quick promotion. Skills in foreign languages are a bonus, especially in the fields of rights and export sales.

Naturally every employer wants speed and accuracy in the main skill of typing and the allied skills of shorthand or audio, but companies rely more and more on audio and wordprocessors. However, many employers are happy with reasonable levels of speed and accuracy if they see a candidate whom they like. The minimum acceptable words-per-minute speeds are usually in the region of 40 to 50 for accurate typing; and 90 to 100 for shorthand (not always obligatory). The graduates who lack the basic skills and who try to get into London publishers via secretarial bureaux are doomed to disappointment.

The salaries offered by publishers in London do not compare favourably with those of most other types of business. But the publishing industry, especially consumer book publishers, offers probably the greatest chance for a secretary to progress to other activities.

Publishers outside London recruit locally from people who are unlikely to have a degree. The chances for such people to advance into other activities (especially in the educational, academic and STM publishers and in particular departments, such as editorial, where the holding of a degree is much emphasized) are much less. They tend to remain on the secretarial ladder, though a few may cross-over.

Although it is quite proper for candidates at interviews to talk openly about their ambitions, those who view the job only as a short-term stepping-stone are unlikely to be taken on. But those who show potential and aptitude may become involved with publishing tasks without bearing responsibility for them. They have the advantage of being in close contact with senior management and if they keep eyes and ears open they are in a position to gain insight into the workings of the company at a high level, knowledge which may come in useful later. They gain that elusive background qualification 'publishing experience'. But as in other careers which depend on a transition between one function and another, there is the risk of getting stuck.

Lastly there is always a demand from publishers for temporary staff to fill jobs vacated by people on holiday or ill. (Thursday is a good day to find work through a bureau.) In London this is a good way of getting the feel of different publishers and can lead to a permanent job.

Responding to advertisements

Advertisements for publishing jobs appear in the trade press (*The Bookseller* and *Publishing News*), in the national press (e.g. the *Guardian*, especially on Mondays and Saturdays, the *Daily Telegraph*, the *Independent* on Wednesdays, *The Times* on Wednesdays, the *Observer*, and the 'Books' section of the *Sunday Times*); in job-related journals (e.g. *Campaign*); and occasionally in specialist journals (e.g. *Times Educational Supplement, New Scientist*). Secretarial vacancies in London appear in the trade and national press, and in free magazines. Publishers outside London may advertise locally. Some publishers use recruitment agencies for jobs needing previous publishing experience.

When an advertisment catches your eye, do not be put off if you fall short of the employer's stated ideal or feel you are on the borderline (and have a compensatory strength), or are just outside the stated age bands.

PREPARING YOUR CV AND COVERING LETTER

To secure an interview you must attract the publisher's attention by submitting an effective and immaculately tailored curriculum vitae and covering letter, without spelling mistakes, inconsistent punctuation or ungrammatical sentences.

The CV is an organized summary of the key facts (not opinions) about yourself. While emphasizing your assets not your liabilities, the CV must be truthful. Each element should prove to the publisher that you have the qualities and skills for the job: omit those that do not. When typed it should take up one or two A4 pages.

For those with short work experience, the chronological CV laid out in a form style is usually the best approach. The information is listed in chronological order under headings.

Under personal details give your full name, contact address(es) with daytime telephone numbers, date of birth **and** age, marital status and nationality. If your home is far from a London publisher preferably quote a southeast address.

The education and training section lists schools etc., with dates, courses taken, grades achieved, special projects, scholarships, prizes. Spotlight any occupational training courses which are relevant or supplemental to the job.

Work experience (e.g. full or part-time, voluntary, overseas, vacation) may be listed in chronological or, if quite extensive or if your last job was directly relevant, in reverse chronological order (i.e. the most recent first), with no unexplained gaps. Provide employers' names, job titles with duties and responsibilities, promotions, special awards, and accomplishments (e.g. ideas that reduced costs, increased profitability, streamlined administration) – one or two short sentences for each job.

If you have worked freelance or run your own business, the work should be described as if you were an employee yet stressing your independence, responsibilities and achievements.

If you have a weak education you may wish to put work experience before education and quote other sources of learning and training. Relevant work outside publishing should be emphasized (e.g. secretarial, office, library, bookshop work, preparing a firm's literature or magazine, proofreading, print buying, compiling mailing lists, public and customer relations, face-to-face selling, accounting, budgeting, computing, teaching, work overseas).

You could reduce the impact of an erratic career of rapid job changes by adopting a functional format: grouping related work under headings and placing the most relevant experience first.

Include a section on skills, especially the practical ones (e.g. wordprocessing/computer literacy, driving, computing, languages, administration, numeracy, public speaking). Try to link skills, particularly those that relate to the job, to work experience, training, membership of societies, professional and trade bodies etc.

Activities and interests may be incorporated under the above heading or listed separately. If you are about to leave full-time education your skills and keen interests (e.g. photography, sport) assume great importance because with little work experience they mark you out. List leadership or administrative positions, and achievements.

The CV ends with the names and telephone numbers of your two or three referees (e.g. your teacher/tutor, or last employer) who can convey your character, stability and competence to perform the job. Brief them beforehand. One should act as a character reference. You can state, if necessary, that they should not be contacted without prior consultation.

CV and letter presentation

Use factual, concise simple language (without abbreviations or jargon) and active verbs. Have someone who is literate or familiar with staff selection to check and edit it.

Use a good quality typewriter, or wordprocessor with letter quality printing or laser printer (use no more than two conventional typefaces and two sizes). If necessary, use a professional typist or bureau.

Use A4 bond paper. Set good margins with adequate spaces top and bottom. Leave one line space between sections. Try not to break a section at the bottom of the first page (a heading should be followed by at least two lines of text, or carried over). Number the two sheets. Insert your name at the top of page two.

Although it is preferable to send the publisher the unblemished first copy on bond paper, a top quality photocopy is acceptable (i.e. black crisp type, white background, no spots, clean edges on good paper).

The covering letter must accompany the CV. Its purpose is to show the publisher the benefits of employing you, to whet the publisher's appetite to learn more about you – to read your CV and to call you to interview. The letter should be no longer than one page of A4, on unlined paper (preferably handwritten legibly in dark ink, especially for jobs involving contact with printers). If you are applying for your first job in publishing you will not have space, nor would it be desirable, to expound at length on your love of books and reading, or on your envisaged contribution to English literature. Do not include gimmicks, such as poetry.

The letter should be addressed to the head of the department to which you are applying, or to the personnel department (or, if replying to an advertisement, to the person stated). Spell the manager's, and the firm's, name correctly. (Check with the receptionist or personal assistant.)

Start with a brief and simple statement of your reasons for writing (e.g. that you are applying for position X, advertised in journal Y, on Z date, or are seeking work) and that you enclose your CV.

Orientate the letter to the job, firm, your suitability and enthusiasm, for example:

- State briefly your current position (e.g. about to leave college with expected qualifications; or currently employed by X firm in Y capacity; or free to start work immediately).
- Show your research of the publisher by referring to recent or future books or promotions etc. If you have yet to enter publishing indicate with evidence your commitment to a publishing career.
- Stress your suitability: relevant experience, skills and enthusiasm. Select the prime ones (you can cross-refer to your CV). Link your attributes to those specified in the advertisement and/or those included in your CV. Convey your enthusiasm by anchoring it to some credential, or a relevant fact.

- Give positive reasons for making the career step and for your keen interest in the job/activity.
- Politely request an interview; say that you look forward to meeting them and are willing to provide more information. You may suggest your availability.
- Sign off 'Yours sincerely' (if Dear Mr/s). If your signature is illegible, print your name underneath.

Use relatively short paragraphs rather than a few long ones; plain English, concise and precise language, and the active voice.

Avoid unappealing abruptness. To judge tone, try reading the letter aloud the next day, or ask someone else to read it. Remember you are trying to persuade a stranger to interview you. Overfamiliarity, casualness and flippancy are out of place but something more than a cold business letter is called for.

Do not challenge the publisher to employ you or regard the publisher as a career counsellor with whom to share fantasies, or someone to be entertained. Do not heap phoney praise on the publisher, indulge yourself in subjective self-praise, confess to past failures, highlight events which may be seen negatively (e.g. 'I am currently unemployed', 'I gave up work seven years ago to start a family'). Never infer that you see the job only as a stepping-stone to further your interests somewhere else.

Completing an application form

Some publishers supply application forms. Make copies of the form. Follow the instructions and read it right through twice before starting. You can still select and emphasize your assets. Take particular care with you full answers to the major open-ended questions or 'other information'. Use the photocopies for drafting and layout. If necessary, attach an extra sheet. You must add a substantive covering letter.

What to do now

Keep the copies of your application(s) close to the telephone(s) you have quoted ready for a call from a publisher. You may receive a rejection – like the majority – or worse, hear nothing. Difficult as it is, do not let depression and frustration colour future applications. No application is wasted: elements can be re-used and modified. Some publishers hold strong but rejected applicants on file.

DIRECT APPROACH TO PUBLISHERS

Many publishing jobs are not advertised, so writing speculatively to publishers can work; but be prepared to write at least thirty applications. Many publishers have high staff turnover at the junior level, and this continually creates new opportunities.

Sending duplicated applications is useless. If you are about to leave full-time education, your CV is likely to be thin on work experience, and the scope for slanting it specifically to a firm limited. However, your covering letter must relate to an individual firm, and be addressed to and relate specifically to a particular manager's department (i.e. write directly to a named manager, reveal your knowledge of the firm and your commitment to publishing, point to your suitability, enthusiasm and realistic contribution to the activity). To ease your workload, target your top five or ten chosen publishers and departments. A stamped-addressed envelope may encourage a reply.

Because so many humanities graduates apply mainly to the London consumer book publishers and to editorial departments, you increase your chances if you apply to other departments. Furthermore, there are many opportunities in specialist areas of consumer book publishing, and in the out-of-London educational/ELT, academic, STM and professional book and journal publishers. It is well worth writing to less well-known small publishers issuing, say around twenty titles per year, and to packagers. There are thousands of intermittent small publishers producing less than five titles per year, which are unlikely to employ staff, though a few may be prepared to offer unpaid work on a project.

Some publishers do not reply to speculative approaches, others hold impressive candidates on file, to be approached later if a job arises. Some will call you for a preliminary discussion which may lead to an interview, or are prepared to offer advice, possibly recommending you for interview in another house. If you hear nothing or receive a letter of rejection, yet are still very keen on that publisher, telephone the manager and persuade him or her to give you a short chat. People whose commitment to publishing is so strong and who persist usually get in.

BEFORE THE INTERVIEW

If you are called to interview, acknowledge quickly. If you decide not to go, say so, and give others the opportunity. Publishers often shortlist between six and a dozen, with possibly a few marginal reserves.

Prepare thoroughly beforehand. **First**, research the publisher, its books or promotions. 'Why do you find them interesting?' This greatly improves your chances.

Second, think of answers to probable questions. As a publisher, what would you be looking for? From your research, you should be able to deal with questions that relate to your interest in the job and test your knowledge of the publisher. Also you should be prepared to discuss what you think are the most important skills needed. You may be asked what you feel would be the most mundane or frustrating parts of the job and how you would cope with them.

The thinking you put into your CV and letter is apposite to questions such as, 'Why do you want to go into publishing?' (don't just say 'I love reading and books') or, 'How is your previous experience applicable?'. 'Why do you think you are suitable?', 'What are your major strengths?' or, 'What makes you think you will be good at it?', and, 'What are your interests or hobbies?'. 'What books do you read?' is asked especially by consumer book publishers. Cite books which correspond to their interests and be prepared to analyse briefly why you think they work.

When asked about your experience be prepared for questions which probe facts, explore your feelings, judgement and motivation. You may well be asked to explain why you left a job. Do not blame the previous employer or specific individuals. Acceptable reasons include: 'I left for a better opportunity' or 'for more challenging work', or 'to broaden my experience'. Redundancy, even if no fault of your own and a common affliction of many in publishing can be related to 'unique' circumstances pertaining to a particular firm. Beware of quoting shortcomings that may be applicable to the job applied for.

You will need to show that you have thought of medium-term career goals, while stressing your preparedness to commit yourself to the job for an effective time-span.

Many new entrants apply, for example to the marketing and sales departments, with the ambition of becoming editors. You may confess that legitimate target to a manager of another department but you must show strong commitment to the job applied for, otherwise you will be rejected.

Book publishing is an ideas business from start to finish. 'What ideas do you have?' may be asked of any applicant in any department. Do not sit dumbfounded. There may be no 'correct' answer – the question is more of a test of initiative and of common-sense.

Third, jot down your own questions. The best ones relate to clarifying features of the job and showing your knowledge of and keen interest in the publisher. Questions relating to the job include its main aspects, what factors promoted its creation, limits of authority, responsibility and independence, whom you would be working with most closely, terms and conditions, future prospects etc. Those relating to the publisher (such as on new developments) could arise from your research. However, you should ask only a few questions – you are the one being interviewed. You could ask questions to which in part you can guess the answer and which will elicit a positive response.

Be careful not to ask questions that are out of your depth, or cheeky or ask the publisher to give you unreasonable special treatment, or that damn you (e.g. 'Well, what books do you actually publish?'). Your questions, or lack of them, many be more revealing than your answers to the publisher's.

Fourth, optional, take samples of printed material on which you have worked (e.g. a college magazine, book, promotional material, sales aids etc.). A powerful visual-aid can focus the interview on your best work. By recounting quickly the brief, the decisions and initiatives taken, the problems overcome, the people involved, you can reveal your analytical, decision-making and organizational abilities, your ideas and effectiveness in dealing with people and your success.

Before the interview, you will need to judge your standard of dress. The style and atmosphere of publishers differs markedly, and some departments, such as accounts, may be more formal than others. Many managers are greatly influenced by the candidate's first impression which, if bad, destroys you. On the whole it is best to appear businesslike and well dressed. Some managers are prejudiced against women wearing trousers.

You must not be late so allow plenty of time, and make sure you know the exact location of the interview. Some publishers are very difficult to find. If you are unavoidably delayed telephone and apologize. On arrival announce yourself to the receptionist and if time allows examine the publisher's material in the showroom. Do not smoke. If you are still waiting, remind the receptionist one minute before the appointment.

THE INTERVIEW

If you are a new entrant, your anxiety may rise outside the interviewer's closed door. While some interviewers will greet you at the door, your first test may be to enter the room confidently (an important skill for most jobs).

You should greet and shake the interviewer's or, if a panel, the Chair's hand, positively. Remember the panel's job titles in order to direct your responses, and do not slouch or smoke. Bring out your letter and CV, with the firm's catalogue displayed (resist irritating hand movements).

Throughout the interview try to amplify and slant relevant assets which reveal your suitability and enthusiasm, anchor your skills to evidence, and ground accomplishments on citing examples, perhaps of a statistical nature. Reveal your research of the publisher, but do not over-praise or lecture.

Maintain eye contact with an interviewer at all times and listen to the questions (politely clarify if necessary). Do not mumble yes/ no answers. Answer questions fully, but judge the length and depth of your reply by watching the interviewer's verbal and non-verbal cues, and interest level. Be prepared for the interviewer's follow-up questions. When stating views make sure your reasoning is sensible and fairly firm, not vague, arrogant or inflexible. Avoid taking extreme positions, especially negative ones.

The danger of talking too much, apart from boring the interviewer, is to go beyond the question and introduce irrelevant facts or opinions either of which inadvertently reveal weaknesses applicable or not to the job. Indeed an interviewer may keep quiet and let you hang yourself. Interviewers tend to form negative impressions more readily, and on less information, than they form favourable impressions; their judgements are apt to be coloured by one or two striking attributes of candidates; and they tend to reject on negatives rather than select on positives (while ignoring irrelevant weaknesses).

The more nervous you become, the faster you may talk. Strive for measured animation. Undue modesty will conceal you, while boasting is damaging. If you have been dishonest in your CV or overstated the case you will be unable to substantiate your claims.

A quality that most interviewers want to see, which can illuminate all others, is enthusiasm. It means having a positive outlook that shines through whatever subject is being discussed.

Finally, the most intangible and important part of the whole exercise is whether the interviewer likes you and thinks you will fit in because most publishers are small businesses and publishing is a personal business. Moreover, some managers set great store on their quality of life expressed by the work they do and the people they have around them.

There are publishers, and/or individual managers, who are anti-union and are careful not to employ activists whom they see as wreckers. On the other hand a candidate's leanings or beliefs may be very desirable to individual managers or particular firms. Some publishers' interests are focused on propagating particular views in society, for example in political, gender, race, religious and health areas. They attract and often overtly seek staff in all departments who are sympathetic to their values.

Having asked your questions, by the end of the interview you should have a clear idea of what the job entails, what will happen next, who will make the next move, and the timescale. Publishers typically use either one or two interview stages.

Not all publishers pay travelling expenses, especially if you live in London and apply to a firm there, or if you are travelling from a great distance. Preferably check with the assistant rather than in the interview.

When the publisher is pretty sure it wants you, your references will be checked. If you receive a letter of rejection it may be advantageous immediately to hand-write a courteous thank you note expressing your acute disappointment and re-affirming your keen interest in the job and firm (you may want to apply for another job in the same firm or you may come across one of the interviewers in another).

If you are the chosen candidate reply quickly if you decide

either to decline or accept the offer. There is usually little or no room for negotiation in junior jobs.

Publishers differ markedly in style of management and atmosphere. As small businesses, the personality of the managing director often has a decisive influence on the whole firm, or (in a large publishing group) on a division of a constituent firm. In some, the managing director is not the dominant personality or is a remote figure. The first months at work are a crucial period for quickly assimilating the politics of the organization and learning how to work within it, how to get things done, how to win and retain the regard of new colleagues. Tactics such as throwing your heart into the new job and being seen to arrive early and leave late will establish an enduring reputation.

POST-ENTRY TRAINING AND NATIONAL VOCATIONAL QUALIFICATIONS

Most people in publishing learn on the job by watching, listening, doing, learning from the successes and mistakes made by themselves, colleagues, and other publishers, and applying that experience to each new project: knowledge is passed on or re-invented. Not many publishers give sufficient emphasis to training. If you are fortunate to work in a firm that trains, take all the opportunities offered. But if not, the initiative is yours to seek out relevant courses and events, to find the time and possibly the money, though the publisher should be persuaded to pay.

Book House Training Centre is the foremost organization in the UK providing training courses to publishers and the content of its courses reflects National Vocational Qualification (NVQ) standards. Additionally, enquire tactfully into people's work in other departments (eventual senior managers acquire an overview of the business as a whole); track talented individuals who may start up new firms or revitalize moribund ones; and build contacts constantly. While hard work establishes your reputation, it is enterprise that puts you in the right place at the right time for the next job.

During the late 1980s, Book House Training Centre (as the lead body for publishing) developed, with the industry, occupational work-based standards or competences for each of the special job categories found in book and journal publishing. These standards form the basis of NVQs. Employees, who have been awarded an

NVQ in their specialized field of work (e.g. editing, design, production, publicity and promotion etc.), have proof that they have attained a defined level of ability in a particular field and that they are competent to do the job to a nationally defined standard. NVQ candidates build a portfolio of work evidence to satisfy an assessor that they have attained the standards. Most of the major publishers have become assessment centres with their own trained and recognized assessors who are themselves externally verified. Assessors are usually managers, experts in the field. Staff in small companies, which choose not to be assessment centres, may be externally assessed. There is also provision for freelances through external centres such as Book House and The Scottish Publishers Association. The Society of Freelance Editors and Proofreaders is encouraging its members to seek appropriate NVQ units.

The introduction of NVQs to the professions has been slow. Book publishing with most of its NVQs at the high level 4 (with management content) is well in advance of most, though the uptake of candidates, initially at least, has been low. Nevertheless, NVQs provide a structured approach to the assessment of staff and further training needs; and may well become in due course a feature of in-house staff appraisal, salary level and eventually of the job market in general. Further information on NVQs in publishing can be obtained from the Publishing Qualifications Board, 344/354 Gray's Inn Rod, London WC1X 8BP, telephone 071–278 4411.

TERMS AND CONDITIONS

Within book publishing there is a great variation in salaries, and no trade-wide statistics are available. However, the National Union of Journalists, which represents some editors, regularly publishes a survey of the rates of pay of firms with which it negotiates as part of its campaign against low pay, and for graded pay structures etc. Traditionally, the many junior jobs in publishing, particularly the editorial, have low starting salaries (sometimes lower than that paid to qualified secretaries), in part a consequence of large numbers chasing few jobs. (Some people argue that the incidence of low pay and the high proportion of female employment at junior levels are not unconnected.)

The law of supply and demand may also affect salary variation across different types of publishing. For example, publishers wanting staff with a humanities background have a large choice and tend to pay lower salaries than legal and medical publishers which may find it very difficult to find staff with the relevant academic qualifications or experience and are thus prepared to pay a considerable premium for them. Moreover, some people like to work in areas which they see as having intrinsic interest and accept lower salaries than if they worked in other fields of publishing. This has applied particularly to those in the literary and prestigious end of publishing. Generally speaking, some main publishers pay middle management salaries which compare favourably to those of the universities.

On the marketing and sales side, salaries have been approaching those of general commerce; but at the top end, the salaries of most marketing/sales directors of publishing companies do not equate with those earned by the heads of large fast-moving consumer goods industries, simply because publishers, even the largest, are smaller enterprises. At the very top, a few of the chief executives earn nearly ten times that of the lowest paid staff.

Four weeks' holiday has tended to become the norm, though sometimes a minimum of three weeks is quoted for new staff, and some companies may offer five or six weeks after many years' service. Whether anyone has time to take all the holiday allowance is another matter.

The terms of a firm's pension scheme (sometimes covering free life insurance), to which employees in some firms contribute say 5–7% of their salaries, become increasingly important to older candidates. A growing number of enlightened publishers give their staff permanent health insurance which could be a far more valuable benefit than life insurance. Some give health insurance free or at reduced rates. Minor benefits include subsidized canteens, or luncheon vouchers, and invariably the provision of buying the firm's books for personal use at cheap prices. (Publishers usually give trade terms to staff of other firms who want to buy their books.)

Though successive governments have drastically reduced the tax advantages of company cars their provision by some publishers to middle management, irrespective of whether they are used for business, is still a benefit and, combined with the salary, can be inducement to people to change jobs.

Compared with many other private sector firms, some publishers score quite highly on maternity leave. Paternity leave and pay may be given sympathetic consideration by some.

Men and women in publishing

There is a very high proportion of women in pre-entry courses and in publishing, particularly London consumer book publishing (by the early 1980s some hardback houses were struggling to raise a cricket team); but the recruitment of women as home sales representatives has lagged behind recruitment in other departments. The significance of the secretarial route into publishing has been an important factor. For some time, however, women have dominated the work of publicity and of rights selling at both junior and senior levels.

Turning to senior management, the directorships on company boards, the picture is the reverse across all kinds of publishing: on the whole men predominate. But in comparison to most other industries in the UK, the elevation of women to company (mainly subsidiary) boards is better, albeit at a slow rate.

CAREER PATHWAYS

In-house editors

Most staff in editorial departments have degrees. In some areas of publishing, such as educational, academic, STM and professional book publishing, the degree subjects (and/or professional qualifications) preferably relate to the specialisms of the lists of books published: however editors deal with many kinds of books outside the narrow confines of the discipline they studied.

Consumer book publishers, too, favour the recruitment of graduates to junior positions. While publishers may argue that a degree in the humanities (especially English literature) is appropriate, others are not too concerned with the subject and think many English graduates make poor desk editors. Although editing has become almost the preserve of graduates, there are young editors without degrees who have attained their positions by direct ascent or circuitous routes.

Like other jobs in book publishing, editorial posts are predominantly filled by people already in the industry, and most people work their way up from or near the bottom. Editorial departments receive more hopeful applicants than any other. The hundreds of humanities graduates who apply to famous consumer book publishers with nothing more than a good degree are, like unsolicited manuscripts, nearly always rejected.

The few advertised posts for junior positions usually say that previous publishing experience is required and many quote the necessity of wordprocessing. Generally speaking, when publishers advertise secretarial posts in editorial departments they want adequate technical attainments. However, there are 'assistant' posts of a quasi-clerical nature in which the skill of typing is a main requirement – such posts are likely to be open to both men and women. The faster the clerical and administrative tasks can be completed, the greater the opportunity of being given more rewarding work, such as proofreading, editing manuscripts or picture research.

The way into editing via secretarial, or assistant work, is common. But, owing to the intense competition for editorial posts, people enter other departments to acquire publishing experience and some cross over to editing. Another, albeit rare, way of entry is to become a researcher employed short-term by reference or highly illustrated book publishers or packagers.

Most editors learn on the job. Smaller publishers occasionally take on people with little or no experience and train them, but large publishers, with so much choice, rarely do. There are, however, sometimes editorial opportunities for those with specialist knowledge in short supply.

Experience which increases a job applicant's attractiveness includes editing school or college magazines, short-term work in a bookshop preferably linked to the area of publishing, knowledge of printing learnt on a course or possibly from amateur experience, or participation in one of the university or college courses on publishing and/or production – a strong asset.

Editing skills and experience may be gained from areas outside conventional bookwork, such as on learned journals (directly relevant to academic/STM/professional book publishers), on illustrated magazines or partworks (directly relevant to highly illustrated book publishers and packagers), on house journals, catalogues and other published material produced by private, public and voluntary sector organizations, and on directories and financial and business publications.

Once inside an editorial department the able normally progress from editing under supervision to desk editing or equivalent, in the same firm or another; or, if progress is blocked, move sideways. To some extent editing skills are transferable to different kinds of publishing, but after a few years staff tend to specialize. Some become specialists in producing highly illustrated books (sometimes moving between publishers and packagers) or children's books; or in broad subject areas of educational, academic, STM and professional books and journals, and so forth.

While some editors leave publishing or are forced out, others cross to other departments or continue desk editing, decide to go freelance, progress to supervising the editing of books in-house or by freelances, or try to get commissioning jobs. The supervisory post of controlling the editing of books is usually a distinct career path – it very rarely leads to commissioning or to the more senior position of editorial director which needs commissioning experience.

The jump to commissioning is big and difficult. There are many junior editors and few commissioning editors. The very skills that make desk editors good – essentially a nit-picking mind which slogs away at the detail – are not in themselves sufficient for the wide-ranging entrepreneurial and risk-taking tasks of commissioning editors who should grasp quickly the general and specific needs of markets and possess the initiative and imagination to chase after and develop authors and books. Junior editors are always overloaded with work (can sometimes feel isolated or become more introverted), are under constant pressure to meet deadlines (especially in learned journals and in packagers), often work beyond office hours and only a few firms give them time to make contacts outside the office. They may, however, help themselves by taking an active interest in the business side, learning from their seniors' successes and failures and, where appropriate, broadening out discussions with authors and establishing a close relationship. Junior editors, especially in consumer book publishing, can develop their editorial judgement by writing reports for seniors on new proposals and monitoring the outcome (some read secretly for editors in other firms). Most editors attain their first commissioning job between their mid-twenties and mid-thirties. While some in their previous jobs may have commissioned books under supervision others have little direct experience. Commissioning editors are overwhelmingly recruited from within publishing, and mainly from junior editors. In learned journal publishing there is some interchange of staff, at both junior and senior levels, between journals and book divisions, and vice-versa. In rare cases people who have wide-ranging contacts or knowledge (such as review journalists or academics) are brought in from the outside and trained in-house. There is also a little cross-movement in consumer book publishing between literary agency, book clubs' editorial or vice-versa. Slightly more significant though is the inward flow of staff from other departments who may cross over at the junior editing level or straight in at the commissioning level from departments such as publicity and promotion (and rights, in consumer book publishing). Moving from a sales job is difficult in consumer book publishing except possibly at the senior level, but easier in educational, ELT, academic and STM publishing where representatives visiting institutions (especially in the ELT and tertiary sectors) build up market knowledge and contacts.

Editors usually stay in their respective areas of publishing: their contacts and market knowledge should become more valuable. When a good editor leaves, the publisher suffers considerable loss of momentum. Management, at least initially, typically want editors to stay for five years, but some editors want to move faster. They may move from smaller firms to larger or from larger to smaller, preferably attaining a more senior job in the process. The acid test of the author–editor relationship is when authors, provided they receive similar terms and treatment, change publisher along with their editors. Editors' reputations spread quite quickly. Those perceived to be successful are courted by other firms. However, editors' overall track records can be unfathomable. Some editors change jobs, possibly wisely, before the full implications of their decisions are reflected in sales records. Consumer book editors, especially if buying in titles from other firms, can build a sound record within a couple of years, whereas textbook editors, especially in educational publishing, take much longer. The timescales of publishing, from commissioning authors through to post-publication, can be a frustration or a salvation.

Higher still, are the even smaller number of editorial directorships or similar. The editors who attain such positions are drawn more and more into management and administration and further and further away from directly publishing books and contact with authors.

Some senior editors who dislike big public companies stay with the independents or become consultants, or literary agents, or freelance editors; or they may establish their own list of books which is marketed and sold by a large company; or they establish with colleagues their own publishing or packaging company. Others manage the publishing operations of large corporations, charities, museums, associations and professional bodies which may encompass retailing and mail-order sales, and co-publishing arrangements with the commercial publishers. A few try their hand at writing while many in their middle age simply disappear.

Freelance editors

Freelance editors are widely used for copy-editing (sometimes on-screen) or proofreading by book publishers and packagers and other organizations, and usually work from home.

Editors go freelance either from force of circumstances – redundancy or single parenthood – or from preference. They have a much greater variety of editing work and like the freedom of working at home without the rigours and costs of commuting to work. Outside the general hubbub of a publishing house, and with fewer interruptions, they may be able to work faster and plan their day to their own rhythm. But forced to maintain a flow of work and pressured to meet deadlines the freelance's day often extends far into the night, to weekends and public holidays.

Before leaving permanent employment, an intending freelance should arrange a house mortgage if necessary (freelances are commonly viewed as a dubious loan risk) and obtain firm offers of work from, say, two or three sources, to cover the following four to six months. Publishers' editors normally look for someone with a minimum of two years' experience in an editorial office. The best ways of obtaining work are through personal recommendation, professional contacts (e.g. through the Society of Freelance Editors and Proofreaders (SFEP), the SYP and WiP or through the National Union of Journalists which maintains a freelance register), or by personal approach to specific in-house editors. Advertising can prove fruitful and so can contacting agencies that organize freelances. A letter to a publisher or agency should have attached a list of previous relevant work, whether as an employee or as a freelance.

A freelance, at the outset, should appoint a qualified account-ant (preferably one recommended by other freelances), essential for dealing with the Inland Revenue over tax-deductible expenses. The first meeting with an accountant should be free.

In-house editors sometimes test prospective freelances. If given a test, it is vital for the freelance to obtain a brief of the kind or level of work expected.

It is useful for freelances to live reasonably close to the pub-lisher, but many operate via the postal service. Many work for only two or three publishers on a regular basis.

Before starting work freelances should ensure that they are adequately briefed, that they receive any house style or style sheet, and that the material is as complete as possible. An in-house editor, having agreed a realistic deadline, may then state a fixed fee for the job. But it is preferable from the freelance's viewpoint to insist on an hourly rate, and to charge as much as the employer is prepared to pay. The highest hourly rates are paid for substantive/re-write manuscript editing, followed by on-screen editing and then 'ordinary' manuscript editing. Proof-reading pays the least. Freelances with specialist knowledge, such as of medicine or law, may receive higher rates than others. The National Union of Journalists recommends hourly rates. Rates higher than normal may be agreed for emergency work that involves evening, weekend or overnight work.

When dealing with an unfamiliar publisher, freelances check initially whether or not additional expenses are paid; and estab-lish the period (e.g. 30 days) within which payment is due. A publisher may, however, want a credit period of 60 days or longer. Freelances should send in invoices at the end of each one-off job, or monthly if regularly employed, even if engaged on a job overrunning a calendar month. Payments overdue should be chased promptly. Freelances should not allow pub-lishers to run up debts – personal contact with the publisher's bought ledger clerk can work wonders.

Indexers

Indexers are mainly freelance and learn their skills either in-house as editors, or as authors, or from studying a course, such as the correspondence course tested by the Society of Indexers.

Picture researchers

Picture researchers acquire a feeling for the job and make contacts by subscribing to the newsletter of the Society of Picture Researchers and Editors and by attending its regular meetings in London. Relevant background experience includes work in a picture agency, art gallery, museum, or library, or as a photographic assistant.

Because so few publishers and packagers are prepared to train, most researchers are self-trained while doing other work – for instance in picture agencies or in a publisher or packager working as a secretary or assistant who obtains pictures from lists supplied. Thus a willingness to learn alone and from others is needed. Although there is no formal pre-entry training, employers should be encouraged to send researchers to one of the short courses.

Those who gain basic training from collecting pictures from lists supplied, may move up within their firms, achieving a greater say in picture selection; or move to others; or go freelance (the job lends itself to working from home). Freelances (most of whom live within commuting distance of London) may carry out assignments for their former employers as well as others. They either approach managing editors or art directors speculatively or more significantly get work through personal recommendation of publishers, packagers and authors. Freelances who work hard can do quite well – many publishers and packagers pay their expenses in addition to an hourly rate equivalent to or well exceeding the rate paid to freelance editors for copy-editing. Though freelances may specialize in subject areas and in books they may also be in demand from partwork and magazine publishers, film, television, video and multimedia companies.

Designers

Design, like production, is an area in publishing where pre-entry specialist training is very desirable. People entering usually have a sound school education up to A level and usually hold a degree or diploma in design. Those without design qualifications may be considered if they have relevant work experience in advertising, commercial studios or at a printers. Some start their careers in publishers' production/design departments as assistants and develop an interest in design. They may study at evening courses, or attend a part-time course.

The design managers of publishers and packagers face a continuous stream of students seeking junior design positions; and aspiring illustrators show their portfolios to design managers, to senior cover designers and, in the case of children's illustration, to the editors concerned with picture books. Managers too actively seek new talent by using their contacts in colleges and by attending exhibitions.

Other factors being equal, the most impressive designers are those who have at college equipped themselves for the commercial world by taking short-term work, preferably concerned with books, and those who have been sufficiently self-motivated and open-minded to carry out their own research beyond the confines of their courses, and those who keep abreast of new technologies, especially in textprocessing, page mark-up, and the electronic creation and manipulation of text and illustration.

Design managers do not have time to go through a lot of irrelevant material. Your main presentation portfolio must not have too much in it, it should be well assembled, sharp, precise and to the point – for example show two, not ten, examples of your best illustrative work. If you have, say, three examples available of one type of design you should have developed the self-critical faculty of choosing the best.

It may be that at art college you have insufficiently covered work at which you will ultimately excel. Many candidates from college applying for junior book designer jobs bring along portfolios crammed with graphics. Design managers are more interested in typography. They want to see at least several designs of books in the form of layouts, grid, type mark-up, prelims and cover design.

Managers are looking for the way in which you solve design problems and the amount of thinking and research you have done. Therefore think through designs beforehand and include the original brief and development phases leading up to a finished design. You may be tempted to show and stress work which in your view has the best finish. More important is the work which shows the best solution – not necessarily the best execution.

You may fear that your main presentation portfolio of selected and relevant material will not do you full justice, so prepare back-up sections easily accessible and containing supporting examples and additional material covering secondary areas.

Finally, do not include in your portfolio other people's work or work on which you have had much help.

At interview, although the presentation of the portfolio forms a key part, your personality may be of equal or more importance. Managers may be looking for a strength yet to be achieved – the way in which you view your work may differ from the way an experienced manager views it. They may try to discover whether you have a particular bent towards illustration or graphic interpretation or typography; whether you have a more analytical or a more creative mind; whether you will get on with editors and whether you will fit in with a design team.

College designers joining publishers for the first time can receive several shocks: there are many staff in editorial, production, marketing and sales, who are designers *manqué*. Only by doing the more boring tasks repeatedly can speed and reliability be increased. The hard discipline of the commercial world is absent from college. Praise received from college lecturers may not be mirrored by design managers. The timescale of book production in which the design phases are separated by months can be frustrating. It takes some time to build a portfolio strong enough to advance your career.

Book designers' skills are generally transferable to different types of publishing. Although some designers move readily across the areas of publishing, many become specialists in one particular type, such as in educational publishing or in the highly illustrated book area (which may overlap with partwork publishing), or in covers.

Generally speaking the more senior designers become, the more they are tied to administration. Most aspire to become art director, design manager etc., but not a managing director: being professional designers foremost, they rarely care to be totally withdrawn from creativity. However, a few opt to team up with an established editor and form a book packaging company, thereby combining close creative involvement with books and the leadership of a firm.

Other designers give up in-house work and develop their freelance assignments, leaving gaps for new entrants and juniors to fill.

Production staff

Production does not require a degree level of education. A good secondary school education with GCSE (or equivalent) mathematics is sufficient so long as candidates are bright enough to pick up work quickly, are willing to learn, and to work alone.

The production assistant/secretarial/administrative support jobs provide the training for a production career, the key to gaining the practical experience, the feel of dealing with suppliers and the base from which to move up. People who begin their publishing production careers at this level can be divided into three main groups.

First, there are those who have a knowledge of production techniques learnt on a course but who have no practical paid work experience and thus need further on-job training. They are educated to A level or even degree level and have completed a short production-related course at a printing college; or a diploma or degree course which encompasses book design and production techniques. Some in this group also have secretarial skills.

Second, there are those who have minimal knowledge of production but have secretarial skills, combined with a good telephone manner. They may be recent school leavers or graduates, and may have or have not worked in another publishing department. (A visit to a book printer stated on a CV reveals an interest in the job.) It is quite possible for a production department to home-grow a production controller from a particularly bright, interested secretary. After a couple of years it is possible to pick up the terminology and gain a fairly broad knowledge of the workings of a publisher, but it is very difficult to learn the job without the basic technical knowledge. Unless they can persuade the publisher to send them on courses, or they themselves attend evening classes, they tend always to be at a severe disadvantage. Nevertheless there are former production secretaries who have worked their way to the top.

Lastly, there are those lucky enough to get an advertised formal traineeship offered by a large production department – unusual in times of recession.

The job of production controller requires usually a minimum of 2–3 years' production experience. When a controller resigns and there is not an assistant with sufficient experience to be promoted, a crisis arises. The publisher must recruit someone with the necessary experience immediately, from another publisher preferably with a similar list, or possibly, at the junior level, from the printing industry.

The job of production manager usually requires a minimum of 3–5 years' production experience, preferably, though not necessarily, with managerial experience. Bearing in mind that new technologies continually affect the ways books are produced and that production managers play a crucial role in their introduction, it is important for candidates to be fully aware of new developments. Without up-to-date knowledge it is impossible to manage a department which is highly technical at one end, and highly administrative at the other.

Production is a fairly distinct career area in which competition is not excessive and gives much responsibility at a young age. It is one of the few departments in publishing where there is a structured way in: the technical knowledge can be acquired by studying a course. A relevant qualification does not unfortunately guarantee a job: it just substantially increases the chances.

The promotional possibilities within a department tend to be less flexible than in an editorial department because the staffing levels and grades relate directly to the number of books produced. Unless a company is expanding, recruitment and promotion depend on staff leaving. Generally, managers favour their own staff provided they have ability, on account of their accumulated knowledge. Because the publishing industry is so small, managers meet at functions and events, know each other and can quite easily check candidates' references. Other potential sources for them are to pump printers' reps and to form links with colleges. Needless to say success in production depends very much on doing a job well and building a good reputation, spread by word-of-mouth, acquiring sought-after knowledge and establishing contacts with suppliers worldwide.

Unlike many other departments, production skills and abilities can be applied across publishing. Production staff can cross the frontiers of different types of publisher. However, some specialize in certain lists which need particular production expertise, namely complex scientific texts and highly illustrated colour books.

Production is a career in itself. While there is some interchange with design, only a few succeed during the first few years of their careers to move into other departments. At the top end some production staff gain board status, some acquire an additional administrative role; some have set up their own firms which provide a production service for publishers, and some cross over to printers or become UK agents of foreign printers.

Publicity and marketing staff

The people working in these areas tend to be fairly young. Many managers attain the posts in their late twenties or thirties, the publicity/promotion assistants in their early to mid-twenties, while below them are the juniors, the secretarial staff. Apart from the specialists – the copywriters, advertising controllers, direct mail specialists (especially those who have worked in mailing houses serving publishers) and designers (who may have work experience outside book publishing), publicity/promotion managers and assistants are recruited predominantly from within book publishing.

The following minimum educational attainments are usually preferred: in consumer book publishing good education up to A level – a degree is not absolutely essential; in educational publishing a degree is highly desirable (in ELT, qualifications or teaching experience in ELT would be an advantage); in academic and professional publishing a degree (or equivalent further educational or professional qualifications) is all but essential, and so is a well-developed intellect. An understanding of why people want to read such books illuminates the way to market them. (In scientific, technical and medical publishing, a science degree is very desirable to a publisher.) Additionally, bearing in mind that publicity/promotion assistants push out a great deal of promotional material and usually attend to their own letters, competent wordprocessing is an absolute must preferably with DTP experience. (Experience of student journalism, of preparing catalogues or bibliographies, would be a plus on a CV.)

Publicity/promotion managers prefer people who have at least one or two years' experience of working in a publicity or promotion department relevant to their type of publishing and thus are familiar with the appropriate techniques, requiring little training. Many of these people gain their foothold by entering departments as secretarial/cum trainee assistants, straight from secretarial college or as graduate secretaries; or they may have crossed at this level from other departments, such as editorial or marketing/sales. Sometimes, depending on the economic climate and company policy, companies of all sizes will take people without experience but young and quick enough to pick up the required techniques. The degree of responsibility encompassed by the job titles ('publicity' or 'promotion assistant') varies, ranging from considerable responsibility for the tasks to working under direction. Another route found in some of the large educational companies (particularly those in the tertiary sector) is to have spent one or two years as a sales representative.

As editorial jobs are so few and far between, people often start in publicity and promotion in the hope of becoming editors. But once embarked in publicity and promotion they find it to their liking: it becomes their career by accident. However, in the early part of one's career, i.e. in the twenties, this area offers flexibility. Indeed, some companies (particularly some of the large non-consumer book companies) regard it (albeit often informally) both as a way in and as a career job, i.e. they would appoint, for example, graduates committed to publishing who would be expected to improve their positions in the industry. Those working in publicity and promotion come into contact with a large number of titles, with people from other industries (the design world, printers, the media), and with senior internal people from editorial and sales, and sometimes from production, rights and distribution. The abilities and learnt skills overlap those of editorial and sales. Thus a few publicity and promotion assistants succeed in moving across (mainly within their companies) to editorial (desk editing or if lucky commissioning); or to sales jobs (straight repping or, if they already have such experience, to the sales management). In consumer book publishing there is also some interchange with rights departments through the overlap in dealing with serial rights. Some publicity and promotion people might view the jobs of desk editing and repping as restrictive, boring or unglamorous in comparison with the variety of their own activities, and look askance at such moves as being sideways or downwards.

However, experience of being a representative is likely to be significant in the long term to anyone aspiring to be a marketing/sales director with full board status. Most of the marketing directors of large and medium-sized companies today were originally sales people who have spent some time selling on the road, home or export (preferably both). Unless publicity and promotion people have such experience they tend to face a career block below the most senior level. But the aspiration of many people is to be a head of a publicity or promotion department, publicizing a list they like, involved with the myriad activities involved in this area; or possibly to start up or join a PR/promotion agency.

Independent PR/promotion

Most agencies are located in or close to London. Such agencies, which are staffed mainly by ex-publishing people, provide services ranging from particular to all aspects of PR and promotion. Only a few are large enough to employ assistants. Their services are offered on a one-off or retainer basis to their clients who are drawn mainly from the consumer book publishers, and sometimes from educational and academic houses. Some agencies also have clients from outside the publishing industry, and some carry out publicity for author clients. Small publishers may use agencies because they lack staff, expertise or contacts. Medium and large houses may use them in a supportive role to their in-house departments, e.g. to cover for a staff shortage due to illness, to overcome the publishing peak in the autumn, or to provide individual attention to a particular book or author which at the time cannot be given in-house.

Home sales

Consumer book reps

The minimum age of reps in medium or large companies is early to mid-twenties. If younger than 23 they need to look older and responsible enough to be taken seriously by buyers. Small companies may employ younger people. A clean driving licence is essential, though a very minor offence might not hinder a strong candidate. GCSE (or equivalent) qualifications may be sufficient, although some companies want A levels and sometimes degrees, but previous selling experience and a bright personality outweigh educational attainment. Strength is necessary to lug the heavy bag from car park to shop.

Publishers want to maintain continuity of contact and trust with their customers. Career reps with many years' experience (provided they do not rest on their laurels) are valuable to their companies. Sales managers of the main companies like to hold on to younger reps as long as they can. They expect them to stay for, say, five years. Although some reps move around territories, it is not advisable for them to change jobs too often. This tends to work against employment opportunities for graduates in some consumer book companies. Over-educated for the job in the medium term, and ambitious, they may be unhappy to stay for what a sales manager considers a reasonable period.

Sales managers look for people with previous selling experience, preferably in the book trade. Small companies are more likely to take on inexperienced and younger reps. Although they do not pay so much as larger companies, they provide the opportunity to learn. It can be tough going. Reps of a small company have fewer books to sell and few of those are likely to set book buyers on fire; nor are there substantial backlists for back-up. But a short spell of under a year should provide just enough calling experience to lift someone off the bottom. Selling experience need not be confined to books.

Bookshop (or wholesale) experience especially of an appropriate type, can provide a way in. Work experience with the large newsagent chains is relevant to mass-market paperbacks, and academic bookselling to academic publishing, carrying in its train the advantage of understanding the companies' books and their markets. By talking to visiting reps they may hear of forthcoming vacancies. But after two years' experience it becomes increasingly difficult to move; eight years would be too long. For those who do manage to cross over to publishing, repping provides the most likely avenue. Another way in is to enter a publisher's sales office in a junior position, or as a secretary, in the hope that a rep vacancy arises. Lastly, very occasionally medium and larger publishers offer specific trainee rep jobs.

A new rep joining a company usually begins in-house to learn about the company and its systems. The forthcoming books and the backlist have to be learnt before a rep goes on the road. A rep without selling experience often spends an initial period under a senior rep, or goes out with the sales manager. Once alone, the new rep will take at least one season to gain the confidence of booksellers and it takes several years to learn negotiating skills and the niceties of dealing with customers, and to discover what is happening in the trade at large.

The usual movement of reps is from one company to another, for example, from small to large. There is some movement between different types of consumer book publishing but it is very rare for a trade rep to transfer to educational repping. Most of the older reps enjoy a lifetime representing a list or publisher that they like, but many under 40 hope for advancement in their own or other companies to an area or regional managership in a large company, or to a sales management position. Reps face a number of special hurdles in career advancement not least of which are fears that retail chains will curtail their visits or that wholesalers will erode their business. Moreover, there are many reps and few opportunities for sales management.

The sales managers, if they are good, tend to stick because their continuity of service is often valued by companies though not necessarily, especially when the sales forces are re-organized. A rep's very success may disincline a sales manager to bring him or her off the road. The majority of reps are isolated geographically from the managements of their companies and thus, out on a limb, their presence goes unnoticed. A rep whose territory surrounds the sales office and who operates out of it does not suffer this particular disadvantage. In order to be noticed a rep really needs to secure a position in a sales office, such as assistant to the manager or as an office manager or in a post selling to the main accounts. For many, such a step would involve moving, probably to London, usually the loss of the car, and possibly lower earnings. Another route is to cross over to export sales, important if aiming to be a sales director. Lastly, there is the transition from rep to sales manager. A good rep unfortunately does not necessarily make a good sales manager. The skills required to organize other people's time, to prompt and direct them, differ greatly from those of the self-organizing lone rep.

In consumer book publishing, reps rarely move to other departments. In theory, starting a career as a rep should be a good foundation in that it swiftly reveals the commercial realities of the market place and shows the type of book that sells. The job also matures people quickly. But in practice moving from being a rep to an in-house department, such as editorial, is very difficult. Reps, cut off from other departmental directors, do not have experience of the internal work of companies and are up against those who have. In this respect junior jobs in marketing (publicity and promotion) are potentially more flexible because even at that level they bring people into contact with senior management. There is another snag. The qualities of aspiring editors do not meet the needs of sales managers who look for people with the skills to sell successfully rather than those whose strengths lie in creative work.

People considering the job of a trade rep should weigh up the compensations and limitations before applying. The car, the expenses, staying in hotels should be weighed against loneliness. The initial excitement of seeing new places, or spending a sunny afternoon in an old cathedral city, should be set against the cold and wet early Monday mornings in a drab industrial town. The job involves much repetition, physical strain and long hours. But it gives great freedom. There is no fixed pattern to the day and nobody sits directly on one's tail.

Educational reps

School textbook publishers recruit their younger reps either, occasionally, from recent graduates (who might have started off in the promotion department) or from ex-teachers (who have the advantages of relevant background and an understanding of what teachers look for in books). (ELT publishers favour TEFL experience and/or qualifications.) Young reps come out of teaching from about their mid-twenties. They may have found their teaching career blocked or perhaps cannot face a lifetime locked in a classroom. (Some reps with teaching experience eventually return to teaching.) The on-job training usually begins with a spell in the sales office or promotion department to gain a feel of the company and the list, followed by a period spent with an experienced rep. It takes about a year to become fully familiar with a long backlist spreading across many subjects at different levels, and to know the competitors' weaknesses.

Historically, educational reps stayed a long time with their companies: the life-long reps who liked being on the road in this sometimes solitary, but free-wheeling type of job had no desire, or found it difficult, to work in an office. But increasingly the ex-teacher reps with sales skills have aspirations, depending on the current state of the job market, of promotion to area or regional reps in large companies, or to sales and promotion management, occasionally to editorial positions.

College reps

The academic and STM publishers who employ reps calling mainly on colleges sometimes take on young graduates. This job provides a marvellous introduction and background to academic/STM publishing. It is personally valuable in that people learn to be self-sufficient and to motivate themselves, and it can provide the base for a marketing/sales or an editing career. The UK subsidiaries of the US-founded college textbook companies have a tradition of promoting some of their reps to in-house positions. However, candidates who have spent several years as reps are attractive to other publishers both for marketing/sales and editing positions. It is possible for these reps to secure junior or full list-building posts, especially if their jobs have included a strong market research element.

Export staff

Unlike some home sales staff of consumer book publishers, new publishing recruits to export sales are usually graduates. However, those without degrees but with foreign languages and/ or work or study experience overseas stand a good chance of employment. New recruits in export sales come from a wide variety of backgrounds, and are not by any means all fresh graduates; nor for that matter do they necessarily have a background in sales or promotion departments of publishers. The experience of living, working, studying or keen interest in overseas countries can clinch a job. That experience would not necessarily have been linked to publishing but would be a further advantage if it were. Examples are work in an overseas bookshop or Voluntary Service Overseas, or English language teaching – the latter two being particularly attractive to educational and ELT publishers.

Routes into export sales commonly start at the bottom. First steps are to become an export sales assistant carrying out office/ secretarial work which may later encompass periods of sales representation overseas, or to become a home or overseas-based sales representative. In the latter case those without any publishing experience start in the sales office to learn the list and systems, and spend time selling books to the home book trade; or additionally, if in educational/academic publishing, promoting books to and in institutions, being sent on export selling courses and accompanying senior staff abroad. Training periods before going solo can last anything from, say, a couple of months to a year. Those already in publishing who have experience of a sales office, or home sales representation, or promotion, and decide to enter export sales may well be able to progress more quickly. While there are publishers who are quite prepared to despatch staff in their early twenties, others prefer the greater maturity and authority of those in their mid-twenties or over.

To reach an export management position, the most important experience to be acquired is selling abroad as a representative or similar. Unless they carry the lists of others, smaller firms cannot afford the great expense of employing staff to travel overseas to the same extent as large firms. Furthermore the major internationally-based publishers periodically offer overseas postings: for instance of short duration covering temporary staff shortages in overseas firms or offices; or medium-term contracts of, say, two to three years, to set up offices. The large firms either train new publishing entrants or take staff from other large publishers or smaller firms that have been unable to give their staff much overseas opportunity. Those posted abroad for several years may not be guaranteed a job on return. However, they are usually in a strong position, if in-house jobs are available, to move to another area of the world, to progress upwards in the marketing/ sales side of the firm, or possibly cross over to commissioning as in ELT publishing; or to gain senior jobs in other firms.

The people attracted to export selling tend to be well-qualified and very ambitious and often want to progress at a faster rate than a publisher can manage. Those who work in export-orientated firms may feel superior to the home sales side. Customers want continuity of contact with one person over many years but UK publishers frequently re-organize. Moreover, once junior staff have gained valuable overseas market knowledge and contacts they may look for advancement inside or outside the company, wishing to take on more responsibility, or areas of the world that generate more turnover, or other publishers' lists that offer better export prospects. Some, set up their own repping business operating out of the UK or abroad, others seek export management positions, or marketing/sales directorships, in publishing or other industries.

Export selling reveals so many different aspects of the publishing business, adds the international aspect and accelerates maturity at a young age. Other factors being equal, those with export experience applying for senior marketing/sales positions have a great advantage over candidates who lack it. Finally, it should be noted that some of the chief executives and senior managers of large international publishers sought overseas experience earlier in their careers.

Rights staff

The selling of rights is a small and specialist career area. Many rights people start as secretaries/assistants in a rights department, but secretaries in other departments – for instance those who have handled contracts – may have an advantage and transfer to a rights department.

Secretaries with imagination who take an overall view and show initiative usually soon have more responsible work (such as handling permissions, drafting selling letters, progressing deals etc.) thrust at them. While some secretaries are never given the opportunity to advance, or do not have the inclination or the aptitude (perhaps revealing a lack of eye for detail), others say, after a couple of years become rights assistants in their own firms or others. The quickest way of building worldwide contacts is by attending international book fairs. It takes several years to get to know faces and form close reliable contacts. Therefore rights assistants need to encourage their firms to send them abroad as soon as possible.

Rights staff tend to specialize in particular rights and may use that expertise to move around publishers. Some attain rights management positions in their late twenties to thirties (though they bring the routine/repetitive work up with them). There is also occasional staff interchange between publishers and literary agencies and vice-versa (e.g. in the selling of translation rights). The prime example of a specialism is in co-edition books, with some movement both ways between highly illustrated book publishers and packagers. (A few export sales staff move into this area.)

Factors which can adversely affect career development are the fluctuating trading conditions which periodically reduce co-edition publishing, the mergers of UK firms, and the growth of internationally owned publishers – all of which impinge on the scope of rights sales.

A good way of enlarging one's contact network and of discussing issues of mutual concern is to join the Rights Circle which holds occasional lunchtime meetings in London.

Distribution, accounts and computing

Traditionally, distribution was regarded by many publishers as the dogsbody end of the business, received little top management attention, and was perceived as a second-rate career area in relation to the publishing side. Such attitudes have rapidly changed in response to escalating costs, pressures from customers for a faster and more reliable service, and the realization that poor distribution loses market share.

People who have taken courses in material handling, work study and physical distribution management, or who have direct experience of consumer goods distribution are particularly attractive. However, a career in book distribution can be founded within publishing from junior positions such as an assistant to the manager, and from the shop floor. The opportunities are considerable because few graduates apply to this important area, and the specialist knowledge and leadership skills acquired can lead to very senior management positions on the service side. It is a relatively distinct career within publishing but allows cross-movement to independent book distributors, retail chain and wholesale (home and export) and book club distribution facilities.

Cross-movement to other publishing departments is difficult owing to the separation of distribution from headquarters. However, junior work on the trade side of order-processing is a quick way of learning a publisher's business and customers: possible side moves would be into home or export sales offices.

The royalties section, similarly, is a specialist career area, but can sometimes be used as a springboard to other areas. Accountants, part-qualified or qualified, can apply their expertise to any industry, and sometimes end up running publishers.

The computer specialists who run publishers' data-processing departments are not tied to publishing. But a new growing area demanding specialist programing, system acquisition and management, is that of electronic textprocessing and graphics manipulation for both book production and related electronic media. Publishers test the current systems to their limits and are only just beginning to exploit them. They will increasingly need in-house specialists. Such people (together with editors and designers) are at a premium. From their technical base, they could within publishing broaden to the creative side of developing new products, or apply their expertise gained within the publishing industry to other industries which are publishers in their own right (e.g. large corporations and financial service industries) and to multimedia firms or consultancies.

Chief executives and managing directors

The top management has traditionally been drawn from former specialist directors – especially editors, followed by people of a sales and marketing background. However, the highest level of major publishers may not necessarily come from within publishing.

CAREER PATHWAYS: AN OVERVIEW

It was mentioned earlier that the first job or jobs within the first few years may not necessarily determine a career path. Many new entrants have little idea of the work of the departments they join and may find they develop a forte and liking for the work. It is possible to move across to other departments and areas of publishing, but over time it becomes progressively more difficult: there are usually candidates who have acquired specialist knowledge of the activity and market knowledge of that particular area of publishing.

In small firms with few staff and less departmentalism it may be easier to move around the firm and learn different jobs, sometimes simultaneously. But such knowledge may not be considered by a larger firm to be specialist enough. In contrast, junior staff in large firms while often finding it more difficult to cross the more pronounced departmental boundaries, may gain in-depth expertise afforded by the greater resources of the publisher. People move from small to large firms (which usually pay higher salaries at the top) and vice-versa: for example, middle-ranking staff of large firms may attain more senior jobs in smaller firms. The promotion of staff (with little direct management experience) to departmental management positions is common.

Unlike huge industrial concerns and the civil service, not even the largest publisher has a big enough staff pyramid to be able to fill staff vacancies from within at the time they occur: internal staff may be thought not to be ready. Publishers are not rash enough to advertise career pathways which cannot be fulfilled but in some large firms there are visible grade progressions within departments.

Although some staff progress upwards in publishers, a few rapidly, it is very rare to spend a whole lifetime with one firm. Rather most people move from one publisher to another, sideways or hopefully in an upward direction. The possibility of getting stuck in any job at any level is ever present.

In moving around companies, most people stay with the type of work in which they have acquired expertise. If moving between activities is far from easy, moving across the major types of publishing is even more difficult. Generally speaking people stay within consumer, or in educational, or in academic, STM and professional book publishing etc. Their expertise is applied to the publishing of books for certain markets and their contacts inside and outside publishing are orientated accordingly.

Some people in their early thirties with much experience want to change direction, for instance, to move from academic to consumer book publishing, or vice-versa. But they are up against people already in that area so their chances of getting a job at the same level of seniority and salary are much more remote. As you increase your expertise of an area the more valuable that expertise becomes and the more difficult it is to throw it aside and turn to something else. There are always exceptions. People do move between departments and types of publishing at all stages of their careers up to and including managing directors but they are in a minority.

Corporate re-organizations and take-overs inevitably affect careers. Employees unfortunately cannot chose their new owners. After a take-over, the acquisitor's staff often enhance their position in the larger organization, whereas the former management of the bought company is realigned: the managers may stay, leave or be downgraded. The more junior staff may leave as the new owners rationalize the departments, for example, by cutting out competing editorial units, sometimes centralizing production and design and rights sales staff, amalgamating the sales forces, centralizing accounting and distribution services, and relocating offices (even across the Atlantic). Many staff who leave with their redundancy payments re-appear in other publishers or go freelance, though some abandon publishing.

Many people in their thirties reach a plateau below management level and fear that their rapidly approaching fortieth birthday is their last chance to make a change. With increasing age the possibilities of movement diminish. However, many senior jobs are filled by people roughly between the ages of thirty-seven to forty-five. After that, unless an individual is particularly well known or brilliant or specialized, changing companies becomes progressively more difficult. By the age of fifty, with the same provisos, it becomes very difficult indeed – there may be no alternative but stay put if possible until retirement age.

Another factor that may constrain intercompany movement is the housing market and your accessibility to a range of firms. House prices in the southeast region tend to be higher and increase at a proportionately faster rate than in the rest of the country; they rise particularly steeply towards the centre of London. If you take a job in a company away from the centre which may offer to pay relocation expenses (and there may be great opportunities in such companies, partly on account of their location) consider the possible career step after that. If you move home too far out, you may be taking a one-way rather than a return ticket.

Staff of commercial publishers are very attractive to the many public, private and voluntary sector organizations operating their own publishing. Moreover, the contacts made and skills learnt in publishing can be applied to other commercial enterprises, not necessarily concerned with publishing.

In publishing, commercial and non-commercial, staff have been traditionally recruited from within the industry; and publishing staff tend to be retained unless they leave voluntarily or are forced out. It has been a relatively closed world. However, with the advent of electronic media markets and the convergence of technologies and accompanying media industries, publishing is opening out. There are now opportunities for people who have distinct skills not only in publishing but also in sound, video and software programming who have the flexibility to apply their skills creatively with others in the evolving electronic publishing mediums. Such people should be at a premium, internationally. Publishing businesses have changed dramatically over the last decades and will continue to do so at accelerating speed.

Appendix: Training for publishers

Book House Training Centre
Book House, 45 East Hill, London SW18 2QZ. 0181–874 2718/ 4608.

A wide range of intensive one- to five-day courses on every aspect of publishing from introductory to senior management level: foundation training, editorial training, publishing and the law, production training, computers in publishing, marketing training, distribution, publishing finance, and management training (see scholarships below). Plus evening classes on copy-editing and picture research.

University of Brighton
University of Brighton, Lewes Road, Brighton, East Sussex BN2 4AT. (01273) 600900.

MA or postgraduate diploma in Fine Art (with Printmaking or Narrative Illustration and Editorial Design specialism).

Falmouth School of Art and Design
Woodlane, Falmouth TR11 4RA. (01326) 211077.

Honours degrees in Graphic Information Design and in Visual Communication. Two-year courses in Copywriting and Art Direction (HND) and Graphic Design (with Typographic Design or Design for Print specialisms) (HND or ND).

Glasgow College of Building and Printing
60 North Hanover Street, Glasgow G1 2BP. 0141–332 9969.

Advanced diploma in Medical Illustration; HNC/HND in Design for Printing; HNC in Electronic Publishing; HNC in Graphic Reproduction; HND in Information and Media Technology with Visual Communications; HNC in Printing Management and Production; HNC/HND in Technical Graphics.

Leeds University
Leeds LS2 9JT. (0113) 431751.

Postgraduate MA in Bibliography, Publishing and Textual Studies.

London College of Printing and Distributive Trades
School of Printing Technology, Elephant and Castle, London SE1 6SB. 0171–514 6500.

Full- and part-time courses: honours degree in Book Production; honours degree in Publishing; postgraduate diploma in Printing and Publishing Studies; ND in Graphic and Typographic Design; ND in Business and Finance (with Introduction to Publishing option); HND in Typographic Design; HND in Business and Finance (with Publishing Management specialism); HND in Design (Bookbinding); diploma in Publishing Production; Craft Bookbinding, Basic and Advanced. Plus a range of short evening classes and one-day seminars on general publishing topics: How to Publish Yourself, Publishing as a Small Business Venture, Publishing as a Career Option, An Introduction to Publishing, Editorial Management, Publishing Management, and several DTP courses.

London School of Publishing
86 Old Brompton Road, South Kensington, London SW7 3LQ. 0171–584 4070.

Evening classes: editorial, magazine editorial, book production, art production, picture research, book commissioning, marketing and promotion, DTP, children's books and contracts and rights.

Loughborough University
Dept. of Information and Library Studies, Loughborough LE11 3TU. (01509) 263171.

Honours degree: Information and Publishing.

Middlesex University
White Hart Lane, London N17 8HR. 0181–362 5000.

BA degree in Writing and Publishing (major/joint/combined) with another subject; postgraduate MA in Computer Integrated Publishing. Small Press Centre runs short courses for self-publishers: Handprinting and the Small Press, Artists' Books, Producing Your Own Publication, Illustrating and Designing by Computer, Business and the Small Publisher, and Outsider Publishing – The Real Freedom of Presses.

Napier University, Edinburgh
Dept. of Print Media, Publishing & Communication, 10 Colinton Road, Edinburgh EH10 5DT. 0131–444 2266.

Four-year honours degree in Publishing.

National Extension College
18 Brooklands Avenue, Cambridge CB2 2HN. (01223) 316644.

Correspondence course in editing.

Nene College, Northampton
Moulton Park, Northampton NN2 7AL. (01604) 735500.

Two-year HND in Design (Print Media Management specialism).

Nottingham Trent University
Burton Street, Nottingham NG1 4BU. (0115) 9418418.

Three-year sandwich HND in Print Media Management; additional full-time year leading to honours degree.

Oxford Brookes University
The Oxford Centre for Publishing Studies, Gipsy Lane Campus, Headington, Oxford OX3 0DP. (01865) 483471.

Joint honours degree in Publishing and another subject; postgraduate diploma in Advanced Studies in Publishing; modular qualifications in a range of subjects with Publishing modules. Evening classes in copy-editing, on-screen editing and book design are organized by the Continuing Education Department, together with a one-day course on computer essentials for editors.

Oxford Publicity Partnership

12 Hid's Copse Road, Cumnor Hill, Oxford OX2 9JJ. (01865) 862763.

One- or two-day courses, mainly for people in marketing departments: Press and PR, Introduction to Journals Publishing, Introduction to Publicity, Copywriting, Printed Publicity for Direct Mail. Of interest to people working in, or interested in, publishing.

Oxford Women in Publishing

c/o Training Matters, 15 Pitts Road, Headington Quarry, Oxford OX3 8BA. (01865) 66964.

One-day courses for women interested in, or working in, publishing: Introduction to Desktop Publishing, Moving into Commissioning, Finance Made Easy, Copy-editing Level I (beginners), Copy-editing Level II (improvers), Introduction to Publishing. Plus a two-day course: Personal Effectiveness – Improving Managerial Performance.

Password Training

23 New Mount Street, Manchester M4 4DE. 0161–935 4009.

One- or two-day courses held in Manchester or London: Foundation, Design & Production, Marketing, Internet.

University of Plymouth

Faculty of Art and Design, Earl Richards Road North, Exeter EX6 2AS. (01392) 475004.

Postgraduate diploma in Publishing and Book Production; MA in Publishing and Book Production.

Reading University

PO Box 217, Reading, Berkshire RG6 2AH. (01734) 875123.

Four-year honours degree, postgraduate diploma and PhD or MPhil in Typography and Graphic Communication.

Robert Gordon University, Aberdeen

School of Information & Media, 352 King Street, Aberdeen AB9 2TQ. (01224) 262963.

Honours degree and distance learning Masters degree in Publishing Studies.

Society of Freelance Editors and Proofreaders
38 Rochester Road, London NW1 9JJ. 0171–813 3113.

A useful range of reasonably priced one-day workshops on practical aspects of publishing for freelances and in-house staff: Introduction to Proofreading; Proofreading Problems; Introduction to Copy-editing; Brush Up Your Copy-editing; Efficient Copy-editing; References; Introduction to Illustrations; Marking Up Manuscripts for Interfacing; Brush Up Your Grammar; Going Freelance and Staying There; Running a One-person Business; Personal Effectiveness. New one-day workshops are a post-beginner copy-editing workshop and an introduction to on-screen editing.

Society of Indexers
38 Rochester Road, London NW1 9JJ. 0171–916 7809.

Open learning indexing course comprising five units. Further optional units are planned. Self-administered tests, formal test papers and tutorial support are available.

Training Matters
15 Pitts Road, Headington Quarry, Oxford OX3 8BA. (01865) 66964.

In-house tailored training in publishing-specific and management skills: Introduction to Publishing; Editing STM Materials; Structuring Editing of Non-fiction; Editorial Planning; Editing for Everyone; Appraisal Training; Coaching Skills for Managers; Finance for Non-financial Staff; Influencing Skills; Management Projects; Negotiating Skills; Personal Effectiveness; Recruitment Practice; Team-building; Time and Self Management. An approved training provider for the Paul Hamlyn Small Publisher Scheme.

University of Sterling
Centre for Publishing Studies, Stirling FK9 4LA. (01786) 473171.

Postgraduate MPhil or diploma in Publishing Studies.

Swansea Institute of Higher Education
Townhill Road, Swansea SA2 0UT. (01792) 203482.

Honours degree in Art and Media Studies (with Publishing and Print specialism).

Thames Valley University
St Mary's Road, Ealing, London W5 5RF. 0181–579 5000.

Honours degree in Information Management (Publishing and Information Studies specialism); postgraduate diploma and MA in Information Management (Publishing).

West Herts College, Watford
Hempstead Road, Watford, Herts WD1 3EZ. (01932) 257660.

Four-year sandwich BSc with honours in Graphic Media Studies (Publishing and Printing or Business Management or Printing and Packaging Technology); postgraduate diplomas in Publishing, in Creative Writing and Copywriting and in Copywriting; HNDs in Typographic Design (also as ND) and in Printing, Publishing and Packaging. Plus distance learning in these areas and short courses on DTP and book, journal and magazine production.

Wolverhampton University
Wolverhampton WV1 1SB. (01902) 321000.

Honours degree in Electronic Media (Design for Print specialism) with one or two other subjects; HND in Design (Electronic Design for Print).

Women in Publishing
Kim Pearl, Training Officer, 94 Fairfax Road, Teddington, Middlesex TW11 9BX. 0181–977 7116.

One-day courses for women on a range of publishing topics: Introduction to Book Publishing, Principles of Marketing, Basic Book Costings, Working Freelance, Selling Rights, The Commissioning Editor's Role, Taking Charge of Your Career, Management Skills, The Author/Publisher Contract, and Editorial Project Management. Plus a weekend residential course, Developing Your Potential.

A number of editorial correspondence courses are advertised regularly in *The Bookseller* and the *Guardian*.

SCHOLARSHIPS

Book House Training Centre

Book House, 45 East Hill, London SW18 2QZ. 0181–874 2718/ 4608.
Administers two scholarships:

- Sir Stanley Unwin Travelling Scholarship – provides funding to research a trade-related project overseas;
- Bertelsmann Scholarship – offers the opportunity for short attachments to a German-speaking publisher or bookseller.

The Paul Hamlyn Foundation

Sussex House, 12 Upper Mall, London W6 9TA. 0181–741 2812. The Paul Hamlyn Foundation, founded in 1965, supports training and education for publishing and bookselling, together with schemes for increasing awareness of books and the publishing industry. A number of different initiatives have been set up (figures as of May 1994):

- A fund has been set up for training grants for small publishers with under 26 employees, to a maximum of £400 per employee, and £2000 per company (1994/95).
- The Foundation has also forged links with two universities, by offering grants of £10 000 each to Oxford Brookes University and the Centre for Publishing Studies at Stirling University which will enable each to offer bursaries towards the cost of course fees to up to 15 students on postgraduate publishing courses who are experiencing financial hardship.
- There is a publishing entry scheme to assist publishers to employ graduates of publishing degree or diploma courses by contributing half of the first year's salary. Vacation work is offered to the student by the publisher concerned.
- Support is given to freelances working for their NVQs.
- The foundation has set up a £10 000 fund to provide training grants to small independent booksellers of £150 per employee

to a maximum of £500 per company. This scheme is administered by the Booksellers Association.

- Grants are also awarded to Book House Training Centre to assist with the publication of *On Course*, and to the Publishing Qualifications Board in support of the introduction of NVQs in book and journal publishing.

The Worshipful Company of Stationers and Newspaper Makers

Administers two scholarships:

- Stationers' Company Major Scholarship Awards – assists young people in publishing, bookselling and related trades with development of their managerial and technological knowledge.
- Stationers' Company Travelling Scholarship – enables management trainees in publishing and related trades to further their education by studying management methods, either in the UK or abroad.

Details from: The Secretary, The Educational Charity of the Stationers' and Newspaper Makers' Company, Inglewood, Oving, Aylesbury, Buckinghamshire HP22 4HD.

Further reading

PERIODICALS

The Bookseller (weekly, J. Whitaker & Sons, 12 Dyott Street, London WC1A 1DF). Essential source of information on publishing and bookselling, with regular special features. Advertisements for jobs in all fields, usually for people with previous experience.

European Bookseller (bimonthly, 3 Queen Square, London WC1N 3AR). Not to be confused with *The Bookseller*; this is a pan-European view of the book trade.

Inprint (monthly). Informative newsletter for young people (Society of Young Publishers, c/o J. Whitaker & Sons, as above).

Logos (quarterly, Whurr Publishers, 19B Compton Terrace, London N1 2UN). Impartial journal providing in-depth examination of book world issues.

Publishing News (weekly, 43 Museum Street, London WC1A 1LY). Thinner and racier than *The Bookseller*, focusing on consumer book publishing and personalities. Runs interesting articles but few job advertisements.

SFEP newsletter (monthly). An excellent newsletter, with useful tips and thought-provoking articles (Society of Freelance Editors and Proofreaders, 38 Rochester Road, London NW1 9JJ).

Wiplash (monthly). Society newsletter for women at all levels in publishing (Women in Publishing, c/o J. Whitaker & Sons, as above).

DIRECTORIES AND REFERENCE BOOKS

Cassell, The Publishers Association and the Federation of European Publishers (annual). *Directory of Publishing, Volumes I and II*. Cassell. Volume I covers the UK, Commonwealth and Overseas; Volume II, Continental Europe. Both provide detailed coverage of mainstream publishers, literary agents, book packagers, trade societies and associations etc., and are updated each year.

Directory of Book Publishers, Distributors and Wholesalers, (annual). The Booksellers Association of Great Britain and Ireland. Annually updated reference book containing key trade information.

Directory of Publishing in Scotland (1993) (3rd edn) The Scottish Publishers Association.

Fishwick, F. (annual) *The Book Trade Year Book*. The Publishers Association. Covers statistical information provided by members of The Publishers Association.

Hall, S. (ed.) (1993) *European Specialist Publishers' Directory*. Gale Research.

Turner, B. (ed.) (annual) *The Writer's Handbook: The Complete Reference for All Writers and Those Involved in the Media*. Macmillan. Packed with interesting information for writers, and hence publishers. Contains 100 pages on UK publishers.

Writers' and Artists' Yearbook (annual). A & C Black. Short entries on publishers and their interests, packagers, literary agents, societies etc.

INTRODUCTORY READING

Bailey, H. S. (1990). *Back in Print: The Art and Science of Book Publishing* (revised edn), University of Texas Press. Penetrating and thought-provoking analysis of the craft and economics of publishing.

Brown, Iain D. *et. al.* (eds) (1991) *The Young Publishers' Handbook*, The Society of Young Publishers. An introductory look at publishing for young people, written by young people in the trade.

Callenbach, E. (1989) *Publisher's Lunch: A Dialogue Concerning the Secrets of How Publishers Think and What Authors Can Do About it*, Ten Speed Press. Aspects of publishing discussed over a series of tantalizing lunches!

Feather, J. P. (1988) *A History of British Publishing* (revised edn), Routledge.

Foster, V. (1993) *Working in Publishing* (revised edn), Careers and Occupational Information Centre.

Legat, M. (1989) *Dear Author: Letters From a Working Publisher to Authors. Prospective and Practised*. Allison & Busby.

Legat, M. (1991) *An Author's Guide to Publishing* (revised edn), Robert Hale. A useful book for publishers to help them understand the author. Also provides practical help for authors in their dealings with publishers.

Lines, J. (1994). *Careers in Publishing and Bookselling* (2nd edn), Kogan Page. Current information on training and careers in the book trade.

McCormack, T. (1988) *The Fiction Editor, the Novel and the Novelist: A Book for Writers, Teachers, Publishers, Editors and Anyone Else Devoted to Fiction*, Sidgwick & Jackson.

Owen, P. (ed.) (1988). *Publishing – The Future*, Peter Owen. An interesting assortment of predictions on where trends will take publishing. Worth reading for a background on how publishing has changed in the last ten years.

Owen, P. (ed.) (1993) *Publishing Now*, Peter Owen. A companion to *Publishing – The Future*. Subtitled as 'A definitive assessment by key people in the book trade'; a collection of essays by people well known in publishing, writing about their own particular fields.

Smith, Ruth *et al.* (1990) *Publishing Business*. Association of Graduate Careers Advisory Services. A slim book introducing publishing as a career.

Stewart, D. M. (1987) *Bluff Your Way in Publishing*, Ravette. A humorous run-down on publishing. Although now containing some out-of-date information, still worth reading.

Unwin, Sir Stanley (1926) *The Truth about Publishing* (revised edn, 1987), Academy Chicago. A new edition of the classic introduction to the bygone era of pre-corporate publishing.

ADVANCED READING, HANDBOOKS AND MANUALS

——(1989) *Harts Rules for Compositors and Readers* (39th edn), Oxford University Press.

——(1992) *International Directory of Printers*, Blueprint Chapman & Hall.

——(1992) *Multilingual Directory of Publishing, Printing and Bookselling*, Cassell and The Publishers Association. Directory of book terminology in seven European languages.

——(1991) *Oxford Dictionary for Scientific Writers and Editors*, Oxford University Press.

——(1991) *Oxford Dictionary for Writers and Editors*, Oxford University Press.

——(1992) *The Print and Production Manual* (7th edn), Blueprint Chapman & Hall.

Balkwill, R. (1994) *Multilingual Dictionary of Copyright, Rights and Contracts*, Blueprint Chapman & Hall.

Bann, D. (1986) *The Print Production Handbook*, Macdonald.

Barnard, M. J. Peacock and C. Berrill (1994) *Blueprint Handbook of Print and Production*, Blueprint Chapman & Hall.

Barlow, G. and S. Eccles (1992) *Typesetting and Composition* (2nd edn), Blueprint Chapman & Hall.

Baverstock, A. (1990) *How to Market Books*, Kogan Page.

Baverstock, A. (1993) *Are Books Different? Marketing in the Book Trade*, Kogan Page.

Bodian, N. G. (1980) *Book Marketing Handbook Volume I*, Bowker.

Bodian, N. G. (1983) *Book Marketing Handbook, Volume 2*, Bowker.

Bodian, N. G. (1984) *Copywriter's Handbook*, Bowker.

Bryson, B. (1994) *Penguin Dictionary for Writers and Editors*, Penguin.

Butcher, J. (1992) *Copy editing: The Cambridge Handbook for Editors, Authors and Publishers* (3rd edn), Cambridge University Press. The indispensable aid for editors and publishers.

Campbell, A. (1993) *The Designer's Handbook* (revised edn), Little, Brown.

Cavendish, J. M. and Pool, K. (1993) *Handbook of Copyright in British Publishing Practice* (3rd edn), Cassell.

Clark, C. (ed.) (1993) *Publishing Agreements: A Book of Precedents* (4th edn), Butterworth.

Davies, G. (1994) *Book Commissioning and Acquisition*, Blueprint Chapman & Hall.

Evans, H. (1993) *Practical Picture Research: A Guide to Current Practice, Procedure, Techniques and Resources*, Blueprint Chapman & Hall.

Evans, H. and Evans M. (1993) *Picture Researcher's Handbook*, Blueprint Chapman & Hall.

Feldman, T. (1990) *Electronic Publishing Perspectives*, Blueprint Chapman & Hall.

Feldman, T. (1993) *Multimedia*, Blueprint Chapman & Hall.

Foster, C. (1993) *Editing, Design and Book Production*, Journeyman Press.

Green, P. (1993), *Quality Control for Print Buyers*, Blueprint Chapman & Hall.

Harris, N. (1991) *Basic Editing: A Practical Course*, Book House Training Centre and UNESCO. A set of text and exercises to teach how to edit.

Harris, N. (1992) *Basic Editing: Practical Exercises*, Spa Books.

Hauser, M. (1990) *The Business of Book Publishing: A Management Training Course*, Book House Training Centre and UNESCO.

Legat, M. (1992) *Understanding Publishers' Contracts*, Robert Hale.

Luna, P. (1992) *Understanding Type for DTP*, Blueprint Chapman & Hall.

Martin, D. (1989) *An Outline of Book Design*, Blueprint Chapman & Hall and The Publishers Association.

Nair, C. (1991) *Book Promotion, Sales and Distribution: A Management Training Course*, Book House Training Centre and UNESCO.

Owen, L. (1994) (2nd edn) *Selling Rights: A Publisher's Guide to Success*, Blueprint Chapman & Hall.

Peacock, J. (1991) *Multilingual Dictionary of Printing and Publishing Terms*, Blueprint Chapman & Hall.

Peacock, J. (1995) (2nd edn) *Book Production*, Blueprint Chapman & Hall.

Sutton, J. and Bartram, A. (1990) *Typefaces for Books*, The British Library.

Tschichold, J. (1975) *The Form of the Book: Essays on the Morality of Good Design* (trans. H. Hadaler; ed. R. Bringhurst, 1992), Lund Humphries.

Williamson, H. (1983) *Methods of Book Design: The practice of an Industrial Craft* (3rd edn), Yale University Press.

Yeo. P. (ed.) (1994) *The DTP Manual*, Blueprint Chapman & Hall.

Index